3 1192 00044 2⌇ W9-AMS-909

INTERIM SITE

MAR 2 5 1980

M.

DRIFTING CONTINENTS, SHIFTING SEAS

AN INTRODUCTION TO PLATE TECTONICS

AN !MPACT BOOK

ILLUSTRATED BY ROD SLATER

FRANKLIN WATTS | NEW YORK | LONDON | 1976

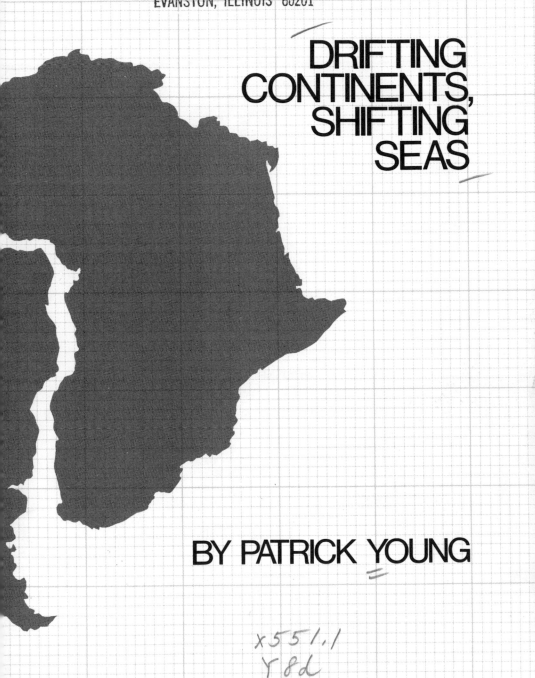

DRIFTING CONTINENTS, SHIFTING SEAS

BY PATRICK YOUNG

Photographs courtesy of: Deep Sea Drilling Project, Scripps Institution of Oceanography: p. 35;
Naval Photographic Center: pp. 46, 56; U.S. De-
partment of the Interior, Geological Survey: pp. 9,
65; Woods Hole Oceanographic Institution: pp. 45,
49, 50.

Library of Congress Cataloging in Publication Data

Young, Patrick.
    Drifting continents, shifting seas.

    (An Impact book)
    Includes index.
    SUMMARY: Introduces that branch of geology
dealing with those forces causing the earth's surface to fold and to move up and down.
    1. Plate tectonics. [1. Plate tectonics. 2. Ge-
ology] I. Title.
QE511.4.Y68   551.1'3   75-40242
ISBN 0-531-00848-7

CONTENTS

For my daughter, Justine

DRIFTING CONTINENTS, SHIFTING SEAS

THE EARTH'S RESTLESS CRUST

Have you ever studied a map of the world and thought that the continents looked like pieces from a jigsaw puzzle? The big bulge of Brazil in South America looks as if it would fit nicely into Africa, hundreds of miles across the Atlantic Ocean. With a little imagination, it isn't hard to see Greenland and Canada nestled up against Europe. And it isn't hard to see the eastern coast of the United States wrapped around Africa from Liberia to the Strait of Gibraltar.

What might surprise you is that nearly all earth scientists (who study the earth—its rocks and its behavior) believe the continents were once joined together in this way. North and South America, Europe and Asia, Africa, Australia, and Antarctica all formed one landmass. Scientists call that continent **Pangaea,** which means "all lands." They believe that Pangaea began splitting apart some 200 million years ago, about the beginning of the age of dinosaurs. If people had ruled the world then, instead of the giant reptiles, they would not have noticed the breakup. The process that split Pangaea apart works very slowly and is called **plate tectonics.** Scientists believe that plate tectonics has been at work for hundreds of millions of years and is still at work. North and South America are moving farther away from Europe and Africa. The Atlantic Ocean is getting wider and the Pacific Ocean is getting narrower.

Tectonics, which means "construction," is a branch of geology (the science that studies the history of the earth by examining its rocks). It deals with the planet's structure, and particularly with the forces that cause the earth's surface to fold and to move up and down. Tectonics has been a part of geology for many years. But plate tectonics, which means the construction of the earth's features by the action of global plates, is a relatively new discovery. It has been in existence only since about the mid-1960s, and it is the most important idea to come along in geology in nearly two hundred years.

For many years, scientists wondered why earthquakes, volcanoes, and mountain ranges occur in distinct and usually narrow belts around the globe. Now plate tectonics provides the answer. Scientists also wondered about the giant underwater mountain ranges that rise from the ocean floor, and the trenches that plunge as deep as seven miles beneath the sea's surface. Plate tectonics explains how these features formed and their importance to our world today.

Plate tectonics shows why fossils of ancient sea life can be found on the tops of mountains. It explains how underground oil pools can exist near the Arctic Circle and how coal deposits can exist in Antarctica, when both of these fuels form in warm climates. Finally, it reveals how enormous continents can wander over the face of the globe.

Earth scientists call plate tectonics a unifying theory, because it answers so many geological questions at once. And by answering them, plate tectonics helps scientists understand the history of the earth and predict more accurately what will happen to our planet in the future.

To understand plate tectonics, you cannot think of the earth's thin, outer shell as a solid, unbroken layer. The earth's crust is cracked in places, and these cracks go very deep. They are not cracks you can see. One cannot look miles and miles into the earth. But the cracks are there. So think of the earth's outer layer as a cracked eggshell. Imagine that the pieces of this cracked eggshell can move about, very slowly. Then imagine that at some cracks material is rising up from inside the egg to create new eggshell. And imagine that at other cracks the shell is being pushed back inside the egg. Now you are beginning to grasp the idea of plate tectonics.

The study of plate tectonics is still very young. Many of the details have yet to be worked out. But enough is known to explain the basic principles, and how they affect those who live on the planet earth.

Earth scientists now picture the earth's outer layer as made up of gigantic, irregular-shaped blocks called plates. These plates move over the globe, carrying continents, islands, and oceans on their backs. They move slowly, only a few inches a year at most. But they move year after year, century after century, millenium after millenium, eon after eon. And as they move, continents pull apart and collide. New oceans are created and old ones destroyed. One of the discoveries in recent years that has amazed geologists is that the entire ocean floor that exists today has been formed in the 200 million years since Pangaea broke apart. Two hundred million years seems a long time. But it is a short period in the history of the earth. Rocks have been found on the continents that are nearly 4 billion years old. And cosmologists (scientists who study the history of the universe) say that the earth itself came into existence some 4.6 billion years ago.

The earth's surface is composed of eight major plates and a dozen or more smaller ones. The major plates are very big indeed. The Eurasian plate carries almost all of Europe and most of Asia, as well as part of the Atlantic Ocean and some of the Pacific Ocean. The North American plate carries the United States (except for the Hawaiian Islands), Canada, Mexico, Greenland, and part of the Atlantic Ocean. The smaller plates are small only by comparison. The Arabian plate, for example, encompasses the entire Arabian Peninsula, and the country of Turkey essentially occupies a plate all its own.

The rigid plates are about fifty miles thick. They are made up of both the earth's crust (the lighter rocks that form the planet's outer few miles) and the uppermost part of the mantle (the denser rocks that lie beneath the crust). This combination of the crust and the upper mantle is called the

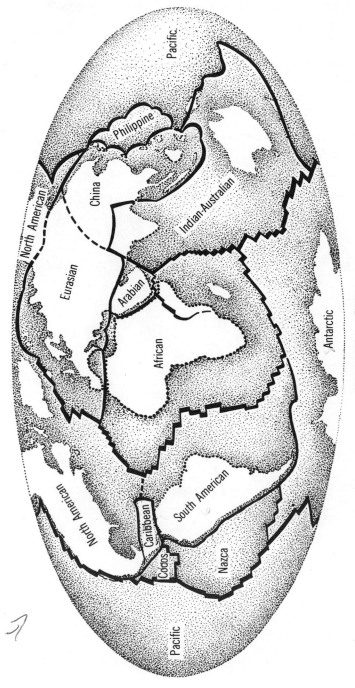

The major plates

Crust

Lithosphere

Asthenosphere

lithosphere. The plates of the lithosphere ride on a less rigid layer of rock called the **asthenosphere.** Rock in the asthenosphere is almost at its melting point.

Most of the world's great mountain ranges and the most destructive earthquakes and volcanoes occur at the boundaries between plates. Great stresses build up in these zones as one plate moves against another. Eventually the stress becomes too great and the rocks snap. This causes an earthquake. If you look at a map of the world upon which seismologists (scientists who study earthquakes) have plotted all the earthquakes that have occurred over eight or ten years, you can clearly see the outline of the earth's great plates. And the famous "Ring of Fire," a line of volcanoes that nearly encircles the Pacific Ocean, outlines a type of plate boundary known as a consuming boundary.

There are actually three types of plate boundaries. Scientists call them accreting boundaries, consuming boundaries, and transform boundaries.

Accreting boundaries occur where plates are moving away from each other. Molten materials, formed within the earth by the melting of rocks in the mantle, seep to the surface to cool and form a new lithosphere. This new material then moves very slowly away from the plate boundary, and new molten rock rises to fill the gap. Almost all the accreting boundaries lie deep beneath the ocean. But an accreting boundary does run through Iceland. That island is slowly growing in size as new rock forms and old rock moves aside.

Consuming boundaries are beneath the sea, too, in the deep trenches of the ocean. There plate material is being destroyed. One plate rides over the top of a second plate and pushes the edge of the second plate back into the earth's interior to be melted. In fact, some of the earth's plates are rather like rocky conveyor belts. Rock rises to the surface in the accreting boundaries. Over millions and millions of years, the rock moves farther and farther away from that boundary. Eventually it reaches a consuming boundary. There it is pushed back into the earth's interior. The rocks that make up the continents, however, are too light to be pushed under. They float along on the lithosphere, like a boat floating along with a river. When continents carried on two separate plates collide, extreme pressures are generated. The ground buckles and folds as a result of the stresses and a new mountain chain is born.

A **transform boundary** exists where the edges of two plates grind past one another. This movement is not smooth. Rocks deep inside the earth fracture and cause earthquakes. A good example is the San Andreas Fault in California. There the Pacific plate, on which Los Angeles sits, is sliding past the North American plate underneath San Francisco. The Pacific plate is inching northwestward. The North American plate is moving toward the southeast. In perhaps 10 million years the area that is now Los Angeles will be alongside where the city of San Francisco now rests.

Plate tectonics is the most exciting and important contribution to geology since the work of James Hutton in the eighteenth century. Hutton was a Scottish geologist. In the late 1700s he developed the idea that the earth's surface is shaped and changed by rain and snow, by rivers and ocean waves, and even by the wind. These everyday forces of nature, he said, worked slowly but surely to wear down mountains, carve deep valleys, and build up layers of dirt called sediments. That meant the planet earth was very, very old, far older than the six thousand years many educated people in Hutton's time thought the world to be. Hutton and the scientists who followed his ideas—notably Scotsmen John Playfair and Sir Charles Lyell—did for geology what Nicolaus Copernicus, Johannes Kepler, and Sir Isaac Newton had done for astronomy. They made geology a modern science.

A section of the 1906
California earthquake fault

The explanation for plate tectonics, however, did not emerge from the mind of a single person. Many scientists in the United States and abroad have helped to work out and explain this important new concept. Their research has forced all the earth sciences to reexamine some of their fundamental ideas, such as how mountains are born. That is why plate tectonics is so vital.

What drives the plates on their wanderings? No one knows. This is one of the great mysteries of plate tectonics. So scientists still call plate tectonics a theory. But as answers are found, earth scientists expect to be able to predict when and where earthquakes and volcanic eruptions will occur. Plate tectonics should also help people locate the petroleum and mineral deposits that our modern world requires.

AN IDEA GROWS

No one knows who first noticed that the continents of the earth looked like parts of a gigantic jigsaw puzzle. **Sir Francis Bacon,** an English philosopher and statesman, noted in 1620 that the lands bordering the Atlantic Ocean looked as if their shorelines matched. But Sir Francis did not suggest that the continents had been joined together. That idea appears first in the writings of a French monk named **François Placet.**

In 1666 Placet suggested that a giant landmass broke apart as a result of the Flood, the forty days and forty nights of rain told of in the Bible. North America separated from Europe, he wrote, and South America split away from Africa during that great deluge.

Placet's idea was echoed nearly a century later in a book by a German theologian, **Theodor Lilienthal.** And in 1800 a German naturalist named **Alexander von Humboldt** argued that the oceans had scoured away land to divide North and South America from Europe and Africa. But few people listened to the idea that continents had once been joined together.

The contraction theory dominated geological thinking during the 1800s. This idea held that the earth was cooling and shrinking in size. This shrinking made the earth's crust crumple and break, which, in turn, caused earthquakes and the formation of mountains. Contraction could alter certain features of the earth's surface, geologists agreed, but the continents and the ocean basins themselves were fixed and permanent. They did not move.

Beginning in 1885, **Eduard Suess** renewed the argument that the continents had split apart. Suess was a brilliant Austrian geologist who continued his work into the early twentieth century. He argued that until about 225 million years ago one large continent existed in the Northern Hemisphere and one or two large continents lay in the Southern Hemisphere. An ocean that he called Tethys separated these lands.

Then in 1910 an American geologist named **Frank Taylor** invoked the idea of moving continents. Taylor believed two large continents once existed. One was at the North Pole and the other was at the South Pole. He suggested that the moon had once been much closer to the earth than it is today. Since the moon was closer, its gravitational pull on the earth—the force that causes ocean tides—was much stronger. In fact, said Taylor, it was so strong that it pulled all landmasses toward the equator. So the two continents —one at each pole—broke apart. Their huge pieces moved slowly toward the equator. Taylor believed that mountain ranges formed when these moving continents ran into each other. For example, he said, the Himalaya Mountains were thrust up when Asia banged into India. In this part of his theory, Taylor proved correct. Mountains are formed when continents collide.

It remained, however, for **Alfred Wegener,** a German-born scientist and Arctic explorer, to set forth the first comprehensive theory of the drifting continents. Wegener was a meteorologist (a scientist who studies the weather) and not a geologist. But he was interested in many things, including flying in the open cockpits of balloons. And he was not afraid to study other areas of science, and think seriously about what he learned. In 1912 Wegener published two articles about his basic theory that all the continents had once been joined together. Wegener called that original continent Pangaea.

Between 1915 and 1929 Wegener expanded and elaborated on his idea in several editions of a small book he called *The Origin of Continents and Oceans.* Wegener's conclusions appealed to some scientists and angered others. Geologists debated his controversial ideas at meetings around the world. Some said Wegener didn't know what he was talking about because he was not a geologist.

As early as 1903, while Alfred was still a student, he had talked about the resemblance between the coastlines of Africa and Brazil. But when he published his theory of continental drift, he relied on far more evidence than the apparent fit of distant coastlines. To bolster his arguments, Wegener drew support from geological data, from the distribution of fossils (the remains of ancient plant and animal life that are preserved in the earth's crust), and from evidence of past climates. It was this ability to draw together many different scientific findings that made Wegener's work so exciting.

Wegener argued that finding the same rock formations in two different places showed that these places once had been joined. And geologists knew of a number of examples. Certain rocks in Scotland match those found in Labrador across the Atlantic Ocean. Rocks along the Ivory Coast of Africa are identical to those found in a plateau in Brazil. And similar geological formations exist in parts of East Africa, on the island of Madagascar, and in India. By matching these and other formations, said Wegener, he could tell where distant lands once had joined together.

Wegener also found evidence in fossils that the same plants and animals had once lived in lands now widely separated by water. Fossils of a primitive fern are found today in both Brazil and Africa. And a type of snail, now extinct, once crawled in both Europe and North America. Again, said Wegener, this was proof that these lands once lay together. His opponents, however, argued that the existence of fossils so far apart could be explained by land bridges— strips of land that rose above the water from time to time to connect the continents. Wegener countered that there was no evidence that such land bridges ever existed.

Finally Wegener turned to evidence that many places had once had climates far different than they have today. He noted that coal is found in Antarctica, and that coal forms from the decay of trees and plants that grow in very warm climates. Wegener also found evidence that trees that now grow in central Europe once dotted the hills of Spitsbergen, a group of Norwegian islands that lie far above the Arctic Circle.

The geological findings, the fossils, and the evidence of past climates spoke to Wegener of only one thing—continents that drifted and moved about the globe. There was no other logical way to explain them, he argued.

Wegener believed that the breakup of Pangaea began about the start of the Jurassic period. (At the time Wegener was writing, the Jurassic period was thought to have begun 40 million years ago. Now the period is dated back to 190 million years ago.) As the continents moved apart, new ocean basins opened. Wegener knew that continental rocks are lighter than the basaltic rocks of the ocean floor. But he argued that the ocean rocks were not as rigid. He envisioned the lighter continents moving through the heavier but more fluid ocean rocks. He compared this movement of lighter rock through heavier rock to icebergs drifting through salty seas.

Wegener encountered his greatest difficulty in trying to explain what force propelled the continents as they wandered over the face of the earth. He suggested two forces were at work. One was a pole-fleeing force that tends to move material toward the equator. The second was the gravitational or tidal force of the sun and moon. Wegener concluded that over millions of years these forces could move the continents.

While both forces do exist, they are extremely small. Wegener's opponents rejected the notion that these tiny forces could drag enormous, rocky continents around, regardless of how many millions of years had passed. As **Harold Jeffreys** of England pointed out in 1924, the earth's own gravity exerts a far stronger force upon our planet's crust than do the sun and the moon. Yet the earth's gravity is not strong enough to flatten mountains or fill in the deep ocean trenches. So the tidal forces of the sun and moon aren't likely to move continents.

Wegener's theory, or "Wegener's hypothesis" as it came to be known, generated intense scientific debate for a decade. By the late 1920s, however, it had been largely rejected. Wegener was a man ahead of his time. As the future would show, he had the correct basic concept. But he failed to persuade most geologists that his theory was right, primarily because he could not explain how the continents moved. This failure (plus some very bad science by some of Wegener's more enthusiastic supporters) led most geologists to dismiss the idea of continental drift. Wegener himself disappeared in 1930 during an expedition in Greenland. He set out on a journey with his dog team on October 30 and was never seen again.

The theory of continental drift did not die out completely with Alfred Wegener on the Greenland ice. A few believers—notably **Arthur Holmes** in Great Britain and **Alexander Du Toit** in South Africa—kept the master's work alive. Yet most earth scientists paid little heed through the 1930s and 1940s. The problem of *how* remained. And it continued to be a mystery until geologists began to examine the ocean floor. There beneath the water lay the answer Wegener couldn't find.

In the early 1950s geologist **Bruce C. Heezen** of Columbia University's Lamont-Doherty Geological Observatory began a project that was to help revive Wegener's theory of continental drift. With **Marie Tharp,** Heezen set out to make pictorial maps of the entire ocean floor. No one had seen what was in the deep ocean, of course. So Heezen and Tharp poured over the echo soundings taken by ships. Echo sounders bounce signals off the sea floor. By measuring how long it takes a signal to make a round trip, scientists can tell how deep the water is. This allows them to chart underwater islands, mountains, plains, and trenches.

Heezen and Tharp started with the North Atlantic, and found an immediate surprise. Oceanographers (scientists who study the ocean and its behavior) knew that some tall feature, which they called the Mid-Atlantic Ridge, existed in the middle of the Atlantic Ocean. But as Heezen and Tharp

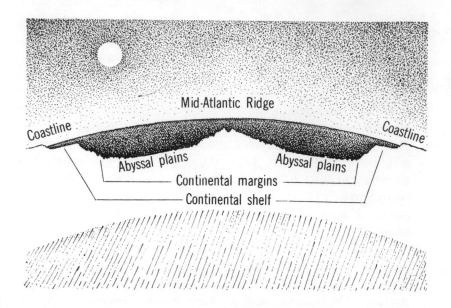

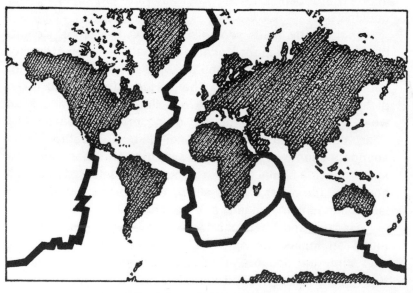

Mid-ocean ridge system

worked, they realized it was not a single ridge, but a wide mountain range that rose from the mid-Atlantic floor. The range is centered in the Atlantic and parallel to the continents on either side of the ocean. The farther away from the middle of the mountains, the deeper the ocean becomes. Then suddenly there are relatively steep cliffs, called the continental margins. And finally there are the shallow waters of the continental shelf, the submerged lands extending out from the coasts of the continents.

As she pondered the echo soundings of the Mid-Atlantic Ridge, Tharp made another discovery. A deep valley ran down the center of the mountain range. Moreover, when she and Heezen compared the location of this valley with a chart of mid-ocean earthquakes, they found most of the tremors took place in or near the valley. They concluded the Mid-Atlantic Ridge held a rift valley, a surface feature that marks a deep crack in the earth's crust.

The two scientists took another look at the records of undersea earthquakes around the world. In places where echo soundings existed, they could see that most quakes occurred along submerged mountain ridges. If that was true, they reasoned, then underwater ridges probably existed in other places where a lot of ocean earthquakes occurred. And then it dawned on Heezen: the Mid-Atlantic Ridge was not merely a large mountain range lying isolated beneath the Atlantic Ocean. It was part of a continuous undersea system of mountains that twisted and turned for 47,000 miles around the world, like the stitching on a giant baseball.

This mid-ocean ridge system runs beneath the North and South Atlantic. It nearly reaches Antarctica, then curves east and swings up into the Indian Ocean. Here it splits in two. One branch runs northward toward India and then shoots off toward the Red Sea, which earth scientists now see as a new ocean in the process of opening. The second branch drops south and then heads east, running between Australia and Antarctica. Far off the coast of South America, the mountain ridges shoot north, ending finally in Mexico's Gulf of California.

A geological feature as enormous as this undersea mountain chain intrigued earth scientists. One of the first to investigate was **Sir Edward Bullard,** an English geophysicist (a scientist who studies the interaction of earth's materials and energy). Early in the 1950s Bullard had begun measuring how much heat flowed up from inside the earth under the ocean floor. When he heard of the work of Heezen and Tharp, he turned his attention to the mid-ocean ridge system. Bullard could not dive into the sea. But by towing a sensitive gauge deep in the ocean, Bullard measured the heat coming to the surface along the ridge system. He found an amazing thing. The temperatures along the ridges were significantly higher than those elsewhere along the sea bottom. Here was evidence that the whole undersea system sat on top of deep cracks in the earth's crust.

While studies of the mid-ocean ridges went on in the 1950s, more evidence for continental drift developed from the work of scientists who specialize in paleomagnetics (the study of the earth's past magnetic activity). The earth is a weak magnet, a fact discovered back in the sixteenth century. It has a north magnetic pole and a south magnetic pole. Invisible lines of force arc between them and make up what is called a magnetic field. The earth's magnetic field has the same shape as the pattern that forms when iron filings are placed on a sheet of glass and a bar magnet is placed underneath.

The earth's magnetic field behaves a bit strangely. Its poles are not located exactly at the earth's geographic north and south poles. They are off by about eleven degrees. The magnetic poles are not stationary. They wander slowly about. And from time to time the magnetic field reverses itself. In the last 76 million years the poles have reversed at least 171 times. And perhaps the most amazing thing is that scientists can find a record of all this magnetic activity frozen in certain rocks.

Many rocks contain iron oxides that can become magnetized and act as tiny compass needles. When these rocks are melted, however, they lose their magnetism. So very hot

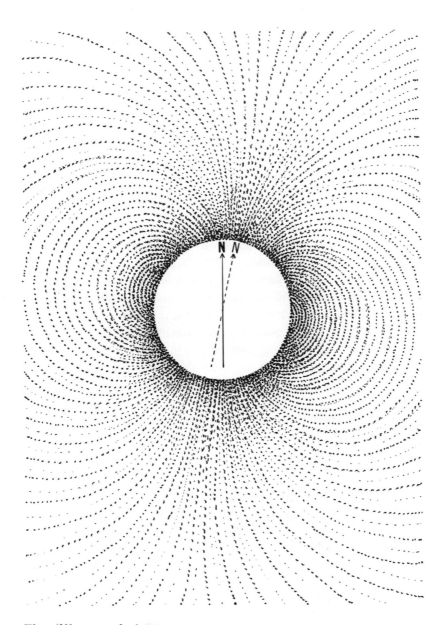

**The difference between
magnetic north-south
and geographic north-south
is called *declination*.**

rock—say, lava from a volcano—shows no magnetism. But as the rock cools, it becomes magnetized in the direction of the north magnetic pole. Most important, the rock retains this record throughout time. A rock magnetized 100,000 years ago will show where the north magnetic pole was then, not where it is today.

In the early 1950s scientists were puzzled by the fact that rocks of the same age on different continents seemed to point to magnetic poles in different places. Rocks of the same age should have pointed to the same place. A group of English scientists, led by atomic physicist **Patrick M. S. Blackett,** concluded in 1954 from its magnetic studies that the British Isles had moved north and rotated clockwise about thirty degrees during the last 200 million years. Soon after that a scientist named **Ted Irving** working in Australia showed that that island continent also had rotated. Finally, **S. Keith Runcorn** and his team at the University of Newcastle upon Tyne in England made a startling announcement. The magnetic records of old rocks in Europe and North America could be explained, they said. All they had to do was to assume the two continents had once been joined together.

Harry H. Hess, a noted geologist at Princeton University, pondered the paleomagnetic studies and the evidence of an undersea ridge system. Increasingly his inquiring mind toyed with an idea he had once thought impossible. Hess concluded Wegener had been right. The continents had moved, and they were still moving. Hess set his ideas down on paper in 1960. He was a careful man who knew that he would be ridiculed by many scientists for accepting the notion of continental drift. And so he called his scientific paper "an essay in geopoetry."

Hess challenged the generally accepted notion that the ocean floor was stationary and permanent. New crust is being created from molten rock pushing up from deep within the earth, he said. The material that rises up in the mid-ocean ridges spreads out to both sides and pushes older material aside. It is a very slow process. Hess estimated that a spot of ocean floor moves only about one half inch a year (a low estimate, as we shall see). The continents, he added, rode along on top of the basaltic rock that formed the sea floor. They are carried along like tin cans on the conveyor belt at a supermarket check-out counter. Hess also concluded that old crust was being destroyed in the deep-ocean trenches.

Hess used a number of arguments to support his idea. For example, he noted that the sea floor's basaltic rock is almost the same depth all over the world. The accepted idea in 1960 was that this sea-floor basalt had spread out from volcanic eruptions. But, said Hess, if volcanoes were the source, the basalt would not be spread out so uniformly. More of it would be piled up at the place where the volcanoes erupted. Hess suggested that instead it was added to the ocean floors along the rifts found in the mid-ocean ridges.

Hess also raised the issue of the sea sediments. The ocean basalt is covered with layers of materials called sediments. They build up from the remains of tiny sea organisms that have lived and died over millions of years and from dirt that is washed and blown into the sea from the land. Hess calculated how deep these sediment layers would be if the oceans were as old as the continents. He decided that from the evidence available the sediments were much too thin. This, he said, was further proof that new ocean floor was being created and old rock destroyed. Hess estimated that the ocean floors were no older than 260 million years.

Although Hess wrote out his ideas in 1960, he did not publish them until 1962. In the meantime, in 1961, a U.S. government geologist, **Robert S. Dietz,** proposed basically the same theory as Hess had evolved. Dietz called the process "sea-floor spreading," a catchy name that quickly came into use. Together, Hess and Dietz stimulated a grand debate that revolutionized the thinking about the earth we live upon.

The science of paleomagnetics had already offered evidence for continental drift when Hess and Dietz advanced the concept of sea-floor spreading. And paleomagnetics

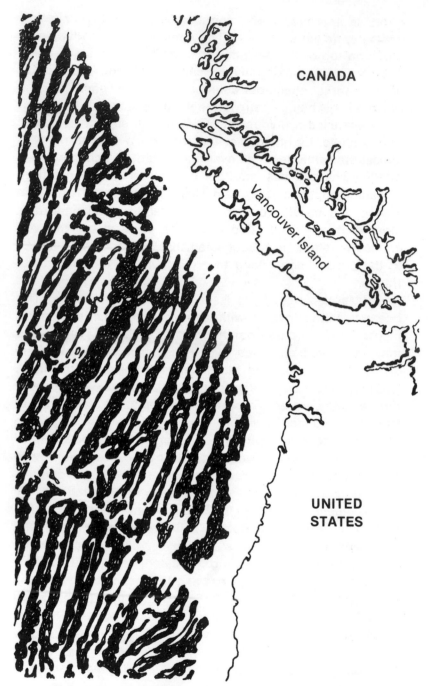

CANADA

Vancouver Island

UNITED
STATES

Magnetic readings forming a zebra-striped pattern.

finally provided the evidence that persuaded many doubting scientists that sea floors did spread and that continents did drift. That evidence came from a pair of English researchers, **Frederick Vine** and **Drummond Matthews.** They found proof where Alfred Wegener could not have looked—deep beneath the sea.

During a scientific voyage off the coast of Oregon and Washington, a British geophysicist named **Ronald Mason** had made a discovery he couldn't explain. Mason was then working at the Scripps Institution of Oceanography in California. He found that magnetic readings from the ocean floor formed a zebra-striped pattern. Some areas gave strong magnetic readings; others gave weak readings. These areas of magnetism alternated—strong, weak, strong, weak— across the sea floor.

Vine and Matthews pondered Mason's findings, and similar magnetic patterns found on the floor of the Indian Ocean in 1962. And then a startling notion occurred to Vine. The magnetic stripes represented reversals in the earth's magnetic poles. They proved the sea floor was spreading.

Vine and Matthews published their ideas in the fall of 1963. They argued that as hot rock oozed up in the mid-ocean ridges and then cooled, it was magnetized. The strong magnetic readings were in rock magnetized when the earth's lines of magnetic force pointed north. The weak readings were in rock magnetized when the lines of force pointed to the south. If new crust was being created in the mid-ocean ridges and moving out on both sides, then a magnetic stripe on one side of the ridge should have a twin on the other side. And this is what further research found. A magnetic area on one side of a mid-ocean ridge has a mirror image on the other side. By careful measurements of the stripes, scientists can determine how fast the sea floor is growing. In some places it averages as little as three quarters of an inch each year. In other places it averages nearly eight inches annually.

The report of Vine and Matthews convinced many scientists that the sea floor was indeed spreading. Other proof followed. Sir Edward Bullard used a computer in 1965 to fit Africa and South America together. Bullard did not use their shorelines. He used the continental margins, which proved to make a much better fit. And **Patrick M. Hurley** of the Massachusetts Institute of Technology used atomic-dating methods (a way of telling a rock's age by measuring the decay of radioactive particles in it) to study rock layers in Africa and South America. He found the pattern of ages of rocks in each continent would fit perfectly if the two continents were joined together.

Also in 1965 **J. Tuzo Wilson,** a Canadian geologist, identified a new type of fracturing of the earth's crust. He called these fractures transform faults, because they occur where an ocean trench or ocean ridge ends abruptly and "transforms" into another feature. Wilson's discovery set the stage for the final formation of the theory of plate tectonics.

By 1967 the idea of sea-floor spreading was winning wide acceptance among earth scientists. It was then that two young scientists working independently added the concept that became known as plate tectonics. **W. Jason Morgan** of Princeton University and **Dan McKenzie** of Cambridge University in England suggested that the earth's crust was divided into gigantic slabs of slowly moving rock that covered the globe like huge paving stones.

The idea of plates was first advanced by J. Tuzo Wilson in 1965. But Wilson envisioned such plates more as mobile belts. Morgan and McKenzie envisioned the plates as rigid blocks of rock. These plates move very slowly in different directions, and they rotate. Hess and Dietz had identified the ocean ridges as boundaries where two plates are moving away from each other. They had seen the ocean trenches as boundaries where one plate forced another back into the earth. Morgan showed that Wilson's transform faults marked a boundary where two rigid plates slipped past each other. Building on the work of many scientists, Morgan and McKenzie put the finishing touches on a unifying theory that explained many geological phenomena—drifting continents, spreading seas, mountains, earthquakes, and volcanoes.

With this broad outline, earth scientists around the world set to work to investigate the important details of plate tectonics. They are still at it, fitting piece after piece into this exciting scientific puzzle.

FROM PANGAEA
TO THE PRESENT

Pangaea was an odd-shaped land. It formed a large, ragged-looking *V* that pointed west like a blunt arrow. Earth scientists call Pangaea's northern arm Laurasia and its southern arm Gondwanaland. Laurasia held what are now the continents of North America, Europe, and Asia. South America, Africa, India, Antarctica, and Australia were all part of Gondwanaland at one time.

The grand movements of the earth's crustal plates, which split Pangaea apart and scattered its continental fragments across the face of the globe, is a slow, slow process. The distance between Europe and North America has increased only about fifty feet in the nearly five hundred years since Columbus sailed from Spain on his voyages of discovery. Yet the movement of the earth's plates is as relentless and as powerful as it is slow. Over millions of years the shifting plates have created new oceans and destroyed old ones. They have built mountains, changed the earth's climate, and influenced the evolution of our planet's animal and plant life.

One important lesson of plate tectonics is that all of the earth's mountain ranges have been formed by plate movements. When two continents collide, the pressures and stresses are tremendous. The earth buckles, and folds, and is slowly pushed up as towering peaks. The Alps of Europe arose because of the repeated pressures of the African and Eurasian plates banging together. It is not just dry land that is thrust upward. As one continent meets another, the

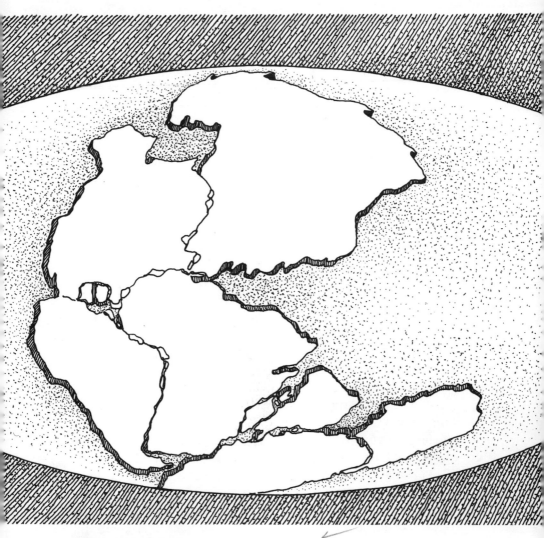

Scientists predict that a
new Pangaea will form some
200 million years from now.
The center of the old Pangaea
will be the coastlines of
the new supercontinent.

ocean between them grows narrower and narrower until it is destroyed. The sea floor is pushed up, carrying with it the layers of sediments that have accumulated over millions of years. That explains why the fossils of ancient sea creatures are commonly found in the mountains.

The moving plates shape the oceans as well. The Atlantic Ocean is growing larger because plates are spreading apart along the Mid-Atlantic Ridge. This pushes Europe and Africa farther and farther away from North and South America.

The Pacific Ocean is getting smaller, because plates under it are being destroyed. These plates spread out from an ocean ridge called the East Pacific Rise. But other plates, such as the South American plate, are overriding the Pacific Ocean plates. The Pacific plates are forced back into the earth and remelted. This process, too, creates mountains. The Andes of South America and the western mountains of the United States and Canada were created by one plate riding over the top of another.

It is impossible to precisely trace the movements of the continents over the 200 million years since Pangaea broke apart. But scientists can map their general wanderings. This is done by reading the record of the earth's magnetic history that is contained in the rocks on the ocean floor. The alternating stripes each represent a reversal of the earth's magnetic field. Scientists can date each and place it back in time. This allows scientists to chart how fast and in what direction various parts of the ocean floor have moved over millions of years. With this information they can trace the basic movements of the continents. Thus they can say with some certainty where the continents were 50 million years ago, 100 million years ago, and 150 million years ago. But the farther back in time one goes, the harder it is to read the magnetic record. So we know more about the earth's continental movements 10 million years ago than about those 100 million years ago.

200 TO 150
MILLION YEARS AGO

The breakup of Pangaea began about 200 million years ago in what is now the center of the Atlantic Ocean. The ocean did not open all at once, in a single, long, jagged crack. The birth of the Atlantic began in two places. Northwestern Africa separated from North America, and a narrow basin opened between what are now Iceland and Britain. At this time North America lay far south of its present location on the globe. Cape Cod was roughly at the equator. Africa and Europe were locked firmly together where the Strait of Gibraltar now lies. About 180 million years ago Antarctica, with Australia attached to it, began breaking away from Africa.

150 TO 130
MILLION YEARS AGO

The South Atlantic began opening about 150 million years ago as Africa and South America split apart along the Mid-Atlantic Ridge. Fifteen million years later, the South Atlantic was still only a narrow sea. But Antarctica, India, Australia, and New Zealand had freed themselves completely from Africa. Europe and Africa had parted, completely separating the two arms of Pangaea's *V,* Laurasia and Gondwanaland. Between them lay a sea that stretched from the Caribbean, through what is now the Mediterranean and Arabia, to the western shores of Indonesia. This long-vanished sea is called Tethys. That is the name Eduard Suess, the Austrian geologist, gave to the ocean he thought divided the continents in the Northern and Southern hemispheres.

130 TO 105
MILLION YEARS AGO

During this period the South Atlantic became a full ocean. North and South America remained separated. And the Bay

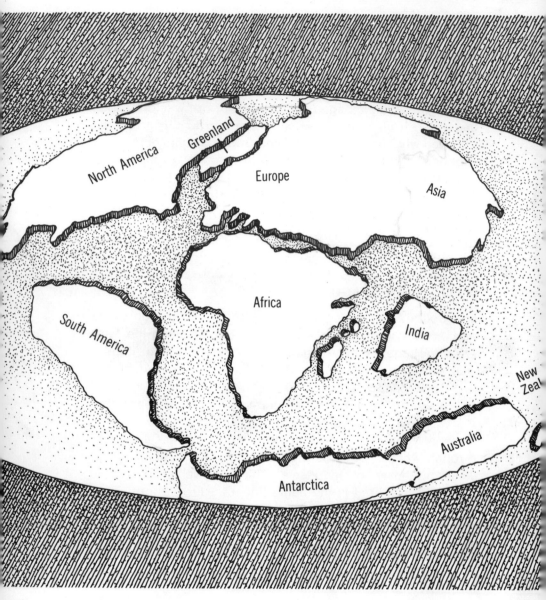

**The location of the
continents approximately
65 million years ago.**

of Biscay formed as the Iberian Peninsula (which now contains Spain and Portugal) wedged into place south of France.

105 TO 65
MILLION YEARS AGO

North America and Greenland separated, and by 85 million years ago the cold Labrador Sea lay between them. Around 80 million years ago New Zealand parted from Australia and Antarctica. Sixty-five million years ago the last part of the Atlantic Ocean began opening between Greenland and northern Europe. Throughout the Atlantic's opening, North and South America had moved farther and farther apart, forming the Caribbean Sea. The two Americas reached their widest separation about 65 million years ago. Then the two continents began moving closer together. So did Europe and Africa about the same time.

65 TO 35
MILLION YEARS AGO

The island of New Guinea broke free from Australia about 50 million years ago. Five million years later Australia separated from Antarctica. Like India before it, Australia began drifting northward. About 45 million years ago the plate carrying India collided with the plate carrying Asia. The result was the birth of the mighty Himalaya Mountains and the world's tallest peak, 29,028-foot Mount Everest.

The Himalayas tower over the world's other mountains. South America's tallest mountain, Aconcagua, stands 22,834 feet above sea level. And only one peak in North America rises above 20,000 feet—the 20,320-foot Mount McKinley in Alaska. The formation of the Himalayas ranks among the epic events in recent geologic time. As India closed in on Asia, it narrowed part of the Tethys Sea, then destroyed it. Sediments that had been laid down upon the continental shelf extending south of Asia were bulldozed before India's re-

(31)

lentless advance. They piled up as the two continents came together, leaving fossils of sea life that lived as long as 150 million years ago scattered north of the mountains, far inland from any ocean.

The Himalayas were not built in a day, or a century, or even a million years. The soaring peaks formed over 45 million years, and they are still growing. Geologists say India's plate has not come fully to rest yet. It is still grinding northward, ever so slowly, inching Mount Everest and its surrounding peaks a tiny bit higher each year.

35 TO 10
MILLION YEARS AGO

By 35 million years ago most of the basic features of the South Atlantic had formed. It was during this period that Italy, once part of Africa, wedged against Europe, adding to the growth of the Alps. Twenty-four million years ago the Amazon River in South America was born, the gradual result of the formation of the Andes Mountains. As the Andes rose, they slowly channeled water from a large area into what became the world's mightiest river. Twenty million years ago the Red Sea opened as Arabia began separating from Africa. Two million years later Africa and Asia joined together in what is now the Middle East. Fifteen million years ago the continuing movement of the African plate against Europe created the Gibraltar Sill, a shallow shelf of rock that lies beneath the entrance to the Mediterranean Sea.

10 MILLION YEARS AGO
TO THE PRESENT

Some time in this period water ceased flowing between the Mediterranean Sea and the Atlantic Ocean. The Gibraltar Sill walled off the Mediterranean and its seawater evaporated. Great pools of brine formed. Then the water evaporated from the brine, leaving thick beds of salt. No one knows how long this process took, but the Mediterranean may have gone from sea to salt flats in as little as one thousand years. Then about five million years ago the level of the world's oceans rose dramatically. No one knows exactly why. But suddenly water from the Atlantic cascaded over the Gibraltar Sill and into the Mediterranean basin. The American geophysicist William B. F. Ryan has estimated that 5 percent of all the water in the world's oceans thundered over a waterfall ten miles wide that lay between the Rock of Gibraltar and Africa. Ryan believes it may have taken only a century to refill the great sea, which stretches from Spain to Asia Minor.

The earth's most recent major geographical change came about 3.5 million years ago. Since the breakup of Pangaea, North and South America had been separated. But then plate movements beneath the Pacific Ocean thrust a strip of land above sea level, creating the Isthmus of Panama, which joined the two continents.

Earth scientists do not yet fully understand the complete history of the continents' movements. Geologists and geophysicists still argue, for example, exactly what continental pieces made up Gondwanaland. (Was Malaysia part of Gondwanaland or not?) They are also millions of years apart in some of their estimates of exactly when various continents broke loose from others. But the pieces of this grand geologic puzzle are being pulled together. The general outline is there. More and more details are being filled in. And since 1968 a remarkable ship called the *Glomar Challenger* has proved invaluable to scientists seeking a clearer understanding of the earth's crustal plates.

The *Glomar Challenger* is a scientific drilling ship, about four hundred feet long. Above its decks towers a drilling derrick, the kind found in oil fields. Special propellers built into the ship allow it to move to one side or another, as well as forward and backward. This is a vital ability. The *Glomar Challenger* roams the world's oceans, working in waters that are far too deep for it to anchor in. Unless the ship can maintain its position precisely over a specific spot for several days, its crew cannot drill into the ocean floor. And this is exactly what the *Glomar Challenger*'s special propellers, special sonar system, and special shipboard computer allow it to do. When a drilling site is chosen, a sonar beacon is dropped to the ocean floor. This beacon sends out sound waves that are picked up by special listening devices on the ship called hydrophones. A computer then automatically controls the propellers, moving the ship one way and then another, so it always remains directly above the sonar beacon and the hole the crew is drilling.

The *Glomar Challenger* can drop its string of drilling pipe down through nearly four miles of water and can core thousands of feet of mud and rocks from the ocean floor. From these samples, geologists find clues that help explain the spreading of the sea floor and the movements of the continents. Drilling so deep through so much water is an amazing accomplishment. It has been compared to drilling a hole in a sidewalk with a string of spaghetti hanging down from the top of the Empire State Building.

The *Glomar Challenger* is financed mostly by the U.S. government and operated by a group of universities. It is named in honor of H.M.S. *Challenger,* a famous British ship that explored the world's oceans in the 1870s. The original *Challenger* measured ocean depths, charted sea-floor contours, and outlined for the first time the general dimensions of the oceans' hidden world. The *Glomar Challenger* has accomplished no less. It has found evidence to support the fundamental principles of plate tectonics.

If new ocean floor is being created at the mid-ocean

The *Glomar Challenger* can hold its drilling position in water up to 20,000 feet deep by means of its sonar sound sources.

DYNAMIC POSITIONING AND RE-ENTRY

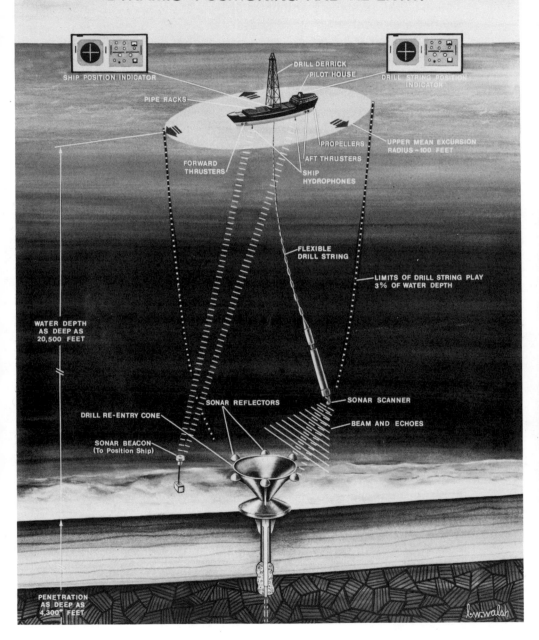

ridges, as Harry Hess argued, then two things must follow. One, the ocean floors must be far younger than the continents. Two, sediments farther away from the ridges will be deeper and older than those nearer the ridges. And this is precisely what the *Glomar Challenger* found. By dating the ages of the fossils found in the sediments, scientists can tell the age of each section of ocean floor sampled by the *Glomar Challenger.* This work proved that sediments near the mid-ocean ridges are younger and shallower than those farther away. And so far, the oldest piece of ocean floor yet recovered is only about 160 million years old. Continental rocks nearly 4 billion years old have been found in Minnesota and in Asia and Africa.

The *Glomar Challenger* drilled the samples that revealed the Mediterranean Sea's history of evaporation and flooding. And on a voyage in the North Pacific, drillings beneath the cold waters off the Aleutian Islands uncovered a type of chalk that forms only in warm, equatorial waters. This evidence showed that part of the Pacific's floor had been moving northwestward for at least 100 million years.

The wanderings of the earth's plates are definitely difficult to decipher. But far harder to unravel is how all this continental movement affected the earth's climate. Consider the ice ages. Did the movement of the continents help create these great advances of polar ice that sent glaciers into the United States? Throughout most of its existence the earth has been largely free of ice. The current situation, where thick ice sheets coat the polar regions of Greenland, is uncommon in geologic history. Perhaps, as a few scientists suggest, the northward drift of the North American and Eurasian plates is responsible. Perhaps their continents reduced the flow of warm seawater from the south into the Arctic Ocean. And perhaps this produced colder weather and more freezing. This is one explanation for the ice ages, but only one. And, as with so many questions about climate, no one knows the answer. Yet as scientists unravel the past wanderings of the continents, they may help climatologists understand the earth's past climates.

Another unanswered question is: Did plate tectonics indirectly cause the demise of the dinosaurs some 65 million years ago? One theory is that the moving plates created climate changes that reduced the vegetation the dinosaurs fed upon. With their food supply disappearing, the great reptiles perished. No one knows if this is what happened. Indeed, there are as many explanations for the vanishing dinosaurs as there are for the coming of the ice ages. But the breakup of Pangaea and the subsequent movement of its rocky fragments did influence the evolution of the earth's plant and animal life.

At the time Pangaea's disintegration began, animals lived throughout the supercontinent. But not all animals lived in all parts of it. With the separation of Laurasia and Gond- wanaland, animals in the north were prevented from moving south, and those in the south were isolated from the north. Eventually meat-eating mammals—tigers, wolves, and bears, for example—developed in the north. So did cattle. To the south, elephants and aardvarks evolved. And in Australia unique forms of life developed, the platypus and kangaroo among them. Australia remained forever isolated. But Eur- asia and Africa reunited some 18 million years ago. And when the Mediterranean was dry, hippopotamuses walked to the island of Cyprus.

Scientists had long known that large bodies of water prevent the migration of animals. Yet the same animals may be found far apart. Lions are found in Africa and India. Bears are found in North America and Europe. Lemurs—small ani- mals resembling monkeys—live in Madagascar, India, and Africa. During the 1800s the idea grew that vast stretches of land, called land bridges, once linked the various continents. Animals migrated across these land bridges, the notion went, but eventually the bridges sank beneath the sea. This con- cept is dead now, killed by our knowledge of the ocean floor. No evidence exists of any great land bridges linking India with Africa, or North America with Europe. Instead, the theory of plate tectonics provides an excellent explanation for the general distribution of the world's animal life.

A dramatic example of animal evolution and redistribution occurred after the Isthmus of Panama rose some 3.5 million years ago. Different forms of mammals had evolved on North and South America after the breakup of Pangaea. George Gaylord Simpson, a paleontologist (a scientist who studies the life of past geological periods), has estimated that twenty-seven families of mammals lived in North America. In South America twenty-nine different families of mammals developed. The Isthmus of Panama allowed these animals to move north and south. The armadillo moved north and established itself. But when animals from North America moved south, particularly meat-eating animals, most mammals of South America could not compete with the invaders. Many South American animals became extinct. And in a relatively short time both North and South America were populated by the same twenty-two families of mammals.

The migration of continents affected more than life on land. It changed life in the sea as well. Most ocean-dwelling creatures live in the shallow coastal waters, at depths of 660 feet or less. The breakup of Pangaea increased the amount of shallow waters available for sea life. And as the continents drifted north and south, different living conditions developed—warmer waters, colder waters, more salt, less salt. This led to the development of a greater number of species. Today the oceans harbor more sea creatures and more different kinds, than at any time in the earth's long history.

The breakup of Pangaea greatly influenced life as we know it on earth. That much is generally accepted, even if the precise details remain unresolved. Indeed, the whole notion of plate tectonics, sea-floor spreading, and wandering continents is generally accepted. But was Pangaea the earth's original continent? Or was Pangaea just a passing episode, a continent itself formed by plate tectonics? The question is still debated, but evidence suggests that plate tectonics has been at work for at least the last 700 million years, and perhaps as far back as 2.2 billion years ago. It is likely, for instance, that Africa's Sahara Desert lay encased in ice 450 million years ago, while North America had a tropical climate. Yet when Pangaea broke apart only 200 million years ago, the two regions lay side by side. Also, several prominent mountain chains are far older than 200 million years—yet they were formed by the same forces that shaped the younger Andes and the Alps.

Trying to trace the earth's geologic history back 700 million years is difficult. But evidence suggests that a single continent existed then, too. It broke apart, and by 570 million years ago four continents were moving about the globe. Sometime about 350 million years ago North America collided with Europe. Over the next 100 million years this collision produced the Appalachian Mountains of the United States and the Caledonian system of Britain and Scandinavia. Some 300 million years ago the landmass carrying North America and Europe joined with Africa and South America. Finally, Asia welded to the rest about 225 million years ago. This collision gave birth to the Ural Mountains and united all of the earth's continents into the single continent of Pangaea.

But the same forces that built Pangaea tore it apart. The restless earth carried Pangaea's crustal fragments through 200 million years into the present. And only now is man coming to understand the mighty geologic process that has shaped his world.

OCEAN RIDGES

We, the people of the world, inhabit only a small portion of our planet. The vast continents and the ocean islands upon which we make our homes cover only about 30 percent of the earth's surface. The rest is ocean. Yet for centuries, people paid little attention to what lay beneath the ocean. They simply had no way of seeing what the sea floor looked like, and only a few people spent any time thinking about it. Those who did concluded that the ocean's floor was flat.

We know differently today. The bottom of the ocean has been sounded, measured, and mapped around the world. Not every inch, or every mile, of course. But enough so that scientists know the basic features of the ocean's 140 million square miles.

The ancients were partly right. Parts of the sea floor are flat, flatter than any island or piece of continent. These immense areas of level ocean bottom are called abyssal plains. They are covered with muddy sediments that may be as thick as several miles. More impressive are the ocean ridges. These broad, rugged mountain ranges generally rise to a height of about seven thousand feet above the abyssal plains, but some of their peaks soar twelve thousand feet or more and are still covered by thousands of feet of water. Ridges are found throughout the oceans, and they occupy a lot of space. If they did not exist—if the ocean floor were all abyssal plain—the sea level around the world would be more than eight hundred feet lower than it is.

The most fascinating ocean ridge is the twisting, continuous system that Bruce C. Heezen recognized in the

1950s. It snakes for some 47,000 miles beneath the world's oceans. It is so long—and parts of it look and behave so differently from other parts—that its various segments have different names. In the Atlantic Ocean the ridge is called the **Mid-Atlantic Ridge.** In the Pacific Ocean it is called the **East Pacific Rise.** In the Indian Ocean one part of the ridge is called the **South-West Indian Rise.** Another part is known as the **Mid-Indian Rise.** And still a third section is called the **Carlsberg Ridge.**

Whatever their names, the segments of the mid-ocean ridge system are vital to plate tectonics. The crests of this system mark the boundaries where various plates are moving away from each other. In the North Atlantic, for example, the North American plate and the Eurasian plate are spreading in opposite directions along the Mid-Atlantic Ridge. Molten material is rising from within the earth to form new crust as the plates separate. Thus the mid-ocean ridge system outlines the accreting boundaries of the plates. It is a volcano 47,000 miles long, whose lava seeps slowly to the surface to form new ocean floor. The American geologist Robert D. Ballard calls the ridge system "the boundary of creation."

The Mid-Atlantic Ridge forms a high, jagged spine down the center of the Atlantic Ocean. At its crest, or middle, is a deep valley, called a rift valley. This valley averages twenty miles in width and drops as deep as five thousand feet below the crest. The Mid-Atlantic Ridge lies deep below the ocean surface, for the most part. But in seven places it rises above the surface to form groups of Atlantic islands.

The East Pacific Rise, though part of the mid-ocean ridge system, is strikingly different. This ridge segment extends from south of New Zealand to the Gulf of California in Mexico. It has no prominent rift valley. Its peaks do not soar as high as those in the Atlantic. The reasons for these differences are the movements of the earth's gigantic plates. The Mid-Atlantic Ridge is spreading slowly, only about one inch a year. The East Pacific Rise is spreading more rapidly

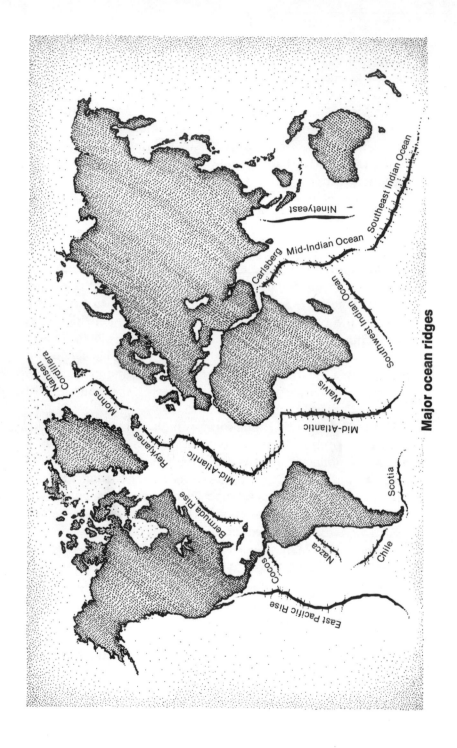

Major ocean ridges

—in some places about seven times faster. Thus the Pacific plates are moving faster and cooling faster than the Atlantic plates. For reasons that earth scientists do not fully understand, only slow-spreading ridges form rift valleys. And the slower the cooling, the higher the ridge grows.

Unlike the Mid-Atlantic Ridge, the East Pacific Rise is not in the center of its ocean. Again, plate movements explain why. The Mid-Atlantic Ridge marks the spot where Pangaea ruptured. North and South America moved westward; Europe and Africa moved eastward. That is why the ridge is in the center of the Atlantic Ocean. But the East Pacific Rise did not split a continent apart. It developed under water, rather than under land. So there is no reason for it to be in the center of the Pacific Ocean.

Earth scientists sometimes speak of the mid-ocean ridges as a window into the interior of the world. If they can understand what is happening at the ridge crests—where material from deep within the planet seeps to the surface— they will learn a great deal about the processes at work inside the earth. But the task is not easy. The exact way in which hot rock finds its way up to form new crust continues to baffle scientists. And trying to solve the mystery is all the more difficult because the activity along the mid-ocean ridges is not identical to anything found on land.

In general, earth scientists believe that cracks called fissures open deep into the earth at an accreting boundary. Material from a huge bulge in the asthenosphere, called a diapir, is pushed upward very slowly by the great pressure inside the earth. This material includes both molten liquid and rock that is hot enough to be pushed like putty through a crack. These hot rocks from the interior are forced up into the fissures. There they cool and weld to the edge of a plate. For some unknown reason, the same amount of new crust welds to each plate. As each plate moves away, new crust is carried with it. New cracks open, and more material rises up from the earth's interior. The whole process is very slow. Along the Mid-Atlantic Ridge each plate adds just about a half inch of new material each year.

The new crust does not cool rapidly. It takes tens of millions of years for it to lose all its excess heat. And this explains, in part, the existence and shape of the mid-ocean ridge system. The hot rock rising at the center expands, but as it slowly cools, it contracts. Therefore those parts of the ridge far away from the crest are lower than those near to it. Finally, when all the heat is lost, the ridge disappears and the sea floor flows along as an abyssal plain. This process also explains the existence of a type of undersea mountain called a guyot. Guyots are believed to be ancient islands that sank beneath the sea as the ridge on which they rode cooled and settled.

Geologists sometimes say they know more about the surface of the moon than they do about the deep-ocean floor. In a sense this is true. Astronomers have excellent photographs of most of the moon, while relatively little of the ocean floor has been photographed. In fact, the first manned dive down to a rift valley did not take place until 1973. In that year French and American scientists made seven reconnaissance dives aboard the French research submersible *Archimède* into the rift valley of the Mid-Atlantic Ridge. They mapped a section of the valley for exploration the following year by Project FAMOUS. (This acronym stands for the French-American Mid-Ocean Undersea Study.)

It is one thing to talk about the great movements of plates and the creation of new crust at accreting boundaries. It is another to dive more than a mile beneath the sea into nearly impenetrable darkness in an attempt to understand these processes. And that is what American and French researchers did in the summer of 1974. They made forty-four dives aboard three submersibles—France's *Archimède* and *Cyana,* and the U.S. navy's *Alvin,* which the Woods Hole Oceanographic Institution operates. The three craft prowled the rugged ocean terrain at depths of 7,200 to 9,600 feet. Usually the scientists could see only 32 to 48 feet, even with their subs' powerful undersea searchlights. One of them said it was "like doing geology at night in a snowstorm with

Archimède

Alvin

a flashlight." Yet their maps and photographs and the rocks they plucked from the sea floor provided strong evidence that new crust is being created along the ocean ridges.

Much of the FAMOUS exploration was concentrated in the deepest part of the rift valley, a two-mile-wide area called the Inner Floor. In the center of the Inner Floor, the diving scientists found several small hills about 650 feet high, which they called the Central High. These hills proved to be small volcanic peaks formed by outpourings of lava. The Inner Floor itself was littered with broken rock, abundant evidence of the valley's earthquake activity. Steep walls bounded the valley on either side, rising as much as 1,000 feet above the Inner Floor.

The research subs also explored two fracture zones, a geologic phenomenon that still puzzles scientists. (Fracture zones were discovered in the 1950s as scientists studied profiles of the ocean floor made by sounding instruments. They are long valleys, most of which run at right angles to the ocean ridges. They point the direction in which rock has been moving away from an ocean ridge.) If you study a map of the Mid-Atlantic Ridge, you find the rift valley is not a single, continuous line. Rather, it looks as if the ridge has been chopped into sections, and the individual pieces slid slightly east or west, along the fracture zones. Some fracture zones extend far beyond the offset sections of the rift valley, measuring sixty miles wide and running one thousand miles or more in length.

Scientists still argue about the meaning of the fracture zones. Some believe they are the remains of ancient trans-form faults. Others have proposed that they formed as the plates made small changes in the directions in which they were moving. Still another view holds that the fracture zones are contraction cracks that result from the cooling of rock as it moves away from the accreting boundary.

As the American and French divers explored the rift valley and the fracture zones, they used clawlike mechanical arms attached to their submersibles to pick up rocks.

The rocks were all basalt, showing they had formed from molten materials. And by the standards of geology, where time is measured in millions of years, the rocks were very young. Two rocks taken from the Central High were less than ten thousand years old. The strangest-looking rocks, ones never found before, the scientists named "toothpaste flows." They are black lavas, tubular in shape, and they look as if they had been squeezed from a tube. The toothpaste flows appear to be pushed from beneath the sea floor to a height of two or three feet. Then they eventually break off. These rocks provide more evidence that rock is pushed up from deep inside the earth at the rift valley.

The tale the Inner Floor rocks tell is complex, but it is important. Although the area where new crust forms is narrow, it is not a simple, single line. Hot rock apparently wells up to the surface across the entire two-mile-wide Inner Floor.

Gliding just above the Inner Floor, American scientists aboard *Alvin* detected more than four hundred cracks, most of them running parallel to the Central High. Some cracks were only inches wide. Others ran forty or fifty feet wide, three hundred feet deep, and a half mile or more in length. *Alvin*'s crews ventured down into several of these fissures to collect samples. Once, while exploring one such narrow fissure, nearly nine thousand feet below the ocean surface, *Alvin*'s pilot found he could not go forward any farther, nor turn to either side. It took him an hour to back *Alvin* safely out of the fissure.

The fissures themselves proved more interesting than the rocks *Alvin* found in them. The cracks suggest that the plates are being pulled apart, rather than being pushed apart. This finding is significant, because it bears on the

The *Alvin*'s mechanical arm
collecting a sample
of "toothpaste" lava

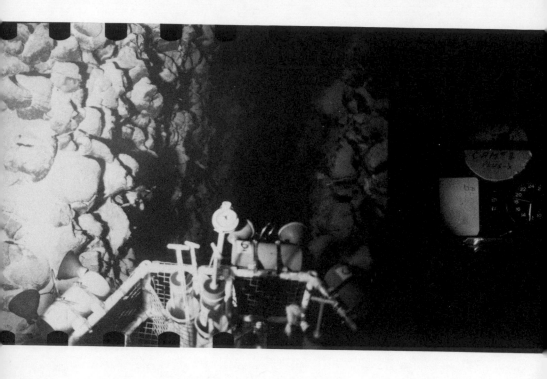

The *Alvin* investigating
a fissure in the
Mid-Atlantic Ridge

biggest mystery of plate tectonics: What drives the plates in their global wanderings?

Essentially, four basic theories have been proposed to explain plate movements.

1. *The plates are forced apart by the upwelling of lava from the asthenosphere.* But the cracks on the Inner Floor found during the FAMOUS dives argue against this. More likely the molten lava seeps passively upward as some other force pulls the plates apart.

2. *Gravity itself is at work.* As the edge of a plate dips back into the earth at a consuming boundary, gravity pulls the rest of the plate after it.

3. *The plates are powered by some heat-driven motion in the upper mantle.* Generally this process is thought to be a form of convection. Convection is the way heat circulates when a liquid or gas is heated. When a pot of water is boiled, for example, the water over the flame rises to the surface. There the water spreads out and cools. As it grows cooler, it becomes heavier, and the water sinks toward the bottom again.

Harry Hess and Robert Dietz both envisioned a slow-motion convection propelling the plates when they outlined their theories of sea-floor spreading. As they described it, molten and semimolten rock rose from deep inside the earth. Some of this rock reached the surface and formed the mid-ocean ridges. But most of the material spread out beneath the plates and slowly carried them away from the ridges. When these convection currents cooled, after tens of millions of years, the rock sank back into the earth's interior, just like cooled surface water sinking to the bottom of a saucepan. Hess and Dietz suggested the ocean trenches marked the places where the convective rocks in the mantle plunged back into the earth.

Today most earth scientists doubt that convection alone moves the plates. There is evidence now that if convection occurs, it takes place only in the upper part of the asthenosphere. And scientists have tried to use models of the earth made of clay and putty to see if convection could drive the plates. They conclude that convection could not occur along a long line like the mid-ocean ridges. So it is unlikely that there is a direct relationship between convective currents in the mantle and any major surface features, such as the ocean ridges.

4. *"Hot spots" or "plumes" drive the plates.* In theory, these are huge pipes or tubes that carry up hot material from deep inside the earth to the surface. J. Tuzo Wilson of Canada initiated the hot-spot concept in 1963 to explain the formation of the Hawaiian Islands. Wilson proposed that a stationary pipe of hot material rose from deep inside the earth beneath the Pacific plate. As the plate moves over this hot spot, the plume of molten material punches through the plate, like a blowtorch through a sheet of steel. Lava flows to the surface and creates a volcanic island. The island of Hawaii now stands over a hot spot, Wilson argued, which accounts for its sometimes violent volcanic eruptions. Additionally, some 3.5 million years ago, the island of Oahu stood over the same hot spot and was created by it. And perhaps 20 million years ago the same hot spot created the island of Midway. As the Pacific plate moved, so Wilson's theory went, it carried each newly created island with it. And then the hot spot punched through the plate again to form another island.

In 1971 W. Jason Morgan drew on Wilson's hot-spot idea and proposed that a number of such spots existed. Morgan had been instrumental in developing the notion that

These drawings demonstrate Wilson's theory of how the Hawaiian Islands were formed.

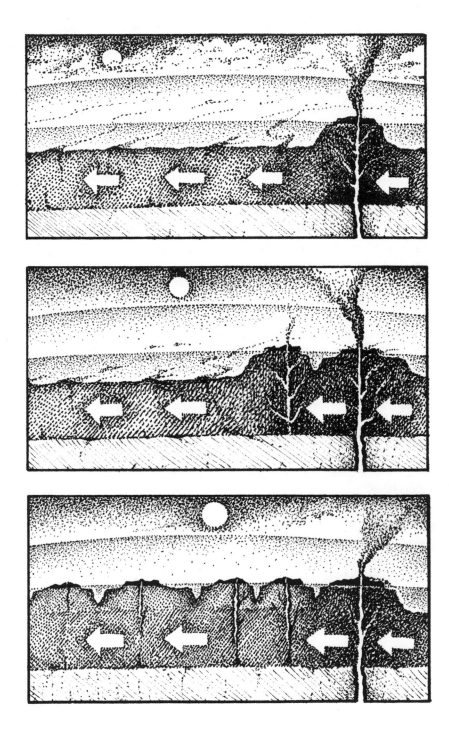

the earth's crust is composed of huge, rigid plates. Now he argued that the plates were powered by giant pipelines of molten materials. These plumes, as wide as sixty miles in diameter, rose from deep inside the earth. They carried up several trillion tons of basaltic rock each year. About 99 percent of this hot material spread out beneath the plates in a circular pattern like a thunderhead cloud. The other 1 percent reached the surface. This spreading out beneath the lithosphere provided the energy to move the plates. Morgan also argued that the hot spots need not be located along the mid-ocean ridges, though many were. Morgan also proposed that the plumes might play a role in creating plates. If several hot spots punched to the surface, the lithosphere between them might break. This would form a crack down to the asthenosphere, and lava could seep to the surface to form an accreting boundary.

A number of scientists find Morgan's theory an intriguing explanation for the mechanism that drives plate tectonics. He and others have now identified twenty possible hot spots around the world. Studies by Peter R. Vogt of the U.S. Naval Oceanographic Office suggest that the plumes do not flow continuously. They seem to turn on and off. Currently, plumes seem to be rising beneath seven island chains along the Mid-Atlantic Ridge. Plume believers argue that these hot spots are responsible for the spreading of the Atlantic Ocean floor. Four other plumes appear evident along the East Pacific Rise.

Not all plumes lie beneath the ocean. Morgan and other scientists propose that the geysers, hot springs, and the earthquake activity in and around Yellowstone National Park result from a hot spot. In 1975 a team of U.S. Geological Survey scientists reported that seismic measurements indicated that a chamber of molten rock, hot liquids, and gases —fifty miles long and thirty miles wide—lies beneath the park. They concluded that Yellowstone may, indeed, be sitting atop a pipeline of hot rock that extends several hundred miles deep, although they can't prove it conclusively.

Another hot spot may be Iceland, which rose some 15 million years ago from the ocean floor. The island is a mountain of lava spewed out of the earth at the point where Greenland and Europe once lay locked together. Iceland's Norsemen, who settled on the island around A.D. 870, found a rugged land of volcanoes, hot springs, and warm earth. For centuries Icelanders washed their clothes in the naturally heated springs and in some areas they even baked their bread by burying the loaves in the hot ground for a day or two. Today almost all the homes in the capital of Reykjavik are heated by water pumped from hot pools beneath the city.

Iceland and its small islands offshore are among the world's most volcanically active areas. Its newest island, Surtsey, burst from the ocean in 1963, a spectacular birth of new earth accompanied by orange lava, stinging cinders, and searing steam.

Nearly ten years later another slumbering Icelandic giant awoke violently. On the night of January 22, 1973, Mount Helgafell on the tiny island of Heimaey erupted for the first time in recorded history. Suddenly, after a few light earthquakes, part of the island split open and fiery lava shot forth. Most of the island's 5,300 inhabitants had to flee to the mainland in the freezing cold of a winter's night. Mount Helgafell's eruption proved an unwelcome reminder to Icelanders that their solidly built homes sit atop vast pools of molten rock.

Iceland is a land of particular significance for scientists studying plate tectonics. It gives them a rare glimpse of the Mid-Atlantic Ridge, for Iceland rests on top of that segment of the global mid-ocean ridge system. Iceland, like the ridge, is the site of new crustal material seeping to the surface. And like the ridge, the island is growing outward from its center. Each year it increases in size by about one inch. The spreading of Iceland is not identical to the spreading that occurs on the sea floor. But the island provides scientists with innumerable clues to plate tectonics.

**The birth
of Surtsey**

Working aboard the research vessel *Trident,* scientists from the University of Rhode Island dredged up volcanic rocks from the Mid-Atlantic Ridge about three hundred miles south of Iceland. In a detailed chemical analysis, the researchers compared these rocks with the volcanic rocks of Iceland. They found a significant difference. The basalt scooped up from the floor of the Mid-Atlantic Ridge originated in the upper asthenosphere. But the rock that formed on Iceland came from far deeper in the earth's interior. This finding was compatible with Morgan's hot-spot idea.

No one yet knows whether hot spots exist, or, if they do, whether they provide the driving force of plate tectonics. Scientists' attempts to understand what moves the plates are seriously handicapped because they simply do not understand the complex processes at work deep inside the earth. And this is what excites so many earth scientists. There is so much to learn, so much to do, to unlock the secrets of our planet earth.

OCEAN TRENCHES

The Pacific Ocean is slowly shrinking. Inch by inch, year by year. One day it may disappear entirely, because the plates carrying Asia and the Americas are moving toward one another. As these plates inch closer, they override and destroy the plates that spread out from the ocean ridge known as the East Pacific Rise.

This is true in the eastern Pacific, where plates carrying South and Central America force the outer edges of the Pacific Ocean's Cocos and Nazca plates back into the earth to be remelted. It is true in the western Pacific, where plates carrying Asia and Australia override the giant Pacific plate. So the great ocean slowly shrinks in size as the plates surrounding the Pacific squeeze closer together.

The places where plates are forced back into the earth are called consuming boundaries. They are marked by deep trenches beneath the oceans, and they make the land features nearby the most geologically active in the world. Most volcanoes and most killer earthquakes occur along consuming boundaries.

Plate tectonics has answered something that had always puzzled oceanographers: Why are the deepest ocean depths found near continents and groups of islands, called island arcs, rather than in the middle of the ocean? The answer is that the ocean trenches mark the place where old crust is pushed back into the earth.

The deepest part of the ocean lies 36,200 feet beneath the surface in the **Mariana Trench** near Guam. Challenger Deep, also in the Mariana Trench, is 35,600 feet deep, and a spot in the **Tonga Trench** in the South Pacific drops 35,400

Ocean trenches

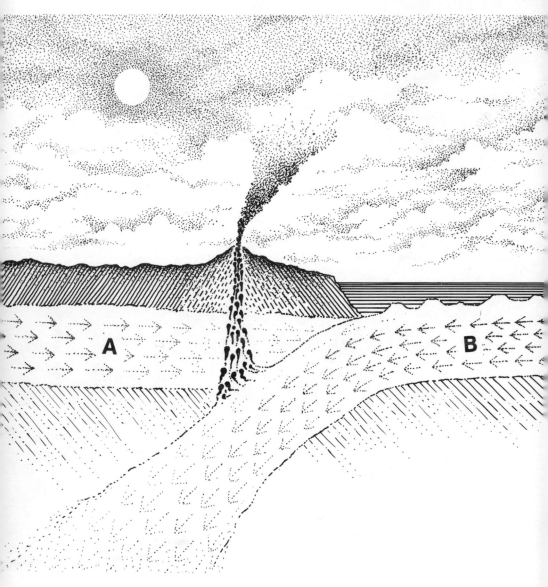

Plate A overrides plate B. As plate B descends, some material melts and rises to the surface as fiery lava.

feet below the surface. The Atlantic Ocean reaches its greatest known depth of 30,200 feet in the **Puerto Rico Trench,** just north of the island of Puerto Rico.

When the edge of one plate rides over the edge of a second plate, it bends the second plate and forces it back into the mantle. This creates a trench in an uneven V shape. The slope of the V that runs toward land is much steeper than the slope on the ocean side. A single trench may run a thousand miles or more in length and measure about sixty miles in width. Typically, it lies a mile or two below the surrounding ocean floor.

The slab of plate that is pushed under by another plate descends at an angle. (Generally this angle is about forty-five degrees, but it may run as shallow as thirty degrees or thrust down almost vertical.) As it sinks deeper, it heats up. But it retains its rigid characteristics to a depth of about 450 miles, nearly one ninth of the way to the center of the earth. At this depth, earth scientists believe, the rock has heated enough to blend in with the surrounding mantle material.

This process, like all plate movements, is slow. It takes about 10 million years for a slab to travel to a depth of 450 miles. Nonetheless, over tens of millions of years a lot of rock can slide down this geologic disposal chute. Scientists believe an enormous segment of the Pacific Ocean floor dropped beneath the western United States as the North American plate moved west. That plate destruction has stopped now. The plate movements have shifted directions, and the deep trench that once lay off the western coast of the United States has vanished. But dormant volcanoes remain as evidence—Lassen Peak in California, Mount Hood in Oregon, and Mount Rainier and Mount Baker in Washington.

Plate destruction plays a vital role in the creation of the rock material that forms the continents. Scientists picture the process beginning at the accreting boundaries. The hot rocks well up from the mantle at the ocean ridges to form ocean floor. They are lighter than the rocks of the asthenosphere. But they are not as light as continental rocks. Nor are they light enough to stay up when one plate is pushed beneath another. But as a plate moves downward, some of its rocks melt at a depth of sixty to one hundred miles. This molten material rises again and forms new continental crust. Most of it cools and solidifies before reaching the surface. But some of it pours out as fiery lava, erupting violently from volcanoes.

The Andes Mountains have formed from volcanoes and the tectonic forces associated with the destruction of the Nazca plate by the South American plate. The famous volcanoes of the Mediterranean, including Etna and Vesuvius, formed from molten rock when the African plate was over-ridden by the Eurasian plate. When Vesuvius burst to life in A.D. 79, after lying dormant for many years, it spewed out lava and ash that killed sixteen thousand people and buried the cities of Pompeii and Herculaneum.

The trenches that almost encircle the Pacific Ocean account for the famous Ring of Fire—the line of active and dormant volcanoes that stretches from western South America through Central America and western North America. The line of volcanoes then swings west along the south coast of Alaska and the Aleutian Islands. It sweeps south again, through Japan, the island arcs of the Pacific, and down to New Zealand.

Some eight hundred volcanoes have erupted during recorded history. About two thirds of these volcanoes are associated with island-arc systems. The most prominent island arcs are in the Pacific Ocean—Japan, the Aleutians, the Philippines, and the Marianas, among them. But there are two in the Atlantic—the West Indies of the Caribbean Sea and the Scotia arc in the South Atlantic.

The islands of an arc are each individual mountains that rise from the sea floor. Generally an arc consists of two gracefully curved and parallel rows of islands. The outer chain of islands is nonvolcanic and is made of sea-floor sediments that have been pushed above the ocean surface. The inner row consists of volcanic peaks.

The volcanic island arcs of the western and northern Pacific are directly related to the volcanoes of today in South and Central America. There are differences, of course. But the volcanoes in both areas lie parallel to deep-ocean trenches. They are located on the plate that is overriding, rather than on that plate that is plunging downward, roughly 60 to 120 miles behind a trench. The **Peru-Chile Trench** lies close to the western coast of South America. But if that trench were far out at sea, the volcanic peaks that now form the Andes would form an island arc instead.

Sometimes, as plates shift their direction of movement, island arcs will be crushed against a nearby continent and become a permanent part of that larger landmass. Some earth scientists believe the eastern United States was formed because North America collided with a series of island arcs long before Pangaea. The island arcs that exist today are young in terms of the earth's history. But the evidence suggests that over the last 2 billion years island arcs have played an important role in shaping the face of the earth. Some researchers even believe they contributed most of the material that now makes up the continents.

The world's largest and most destructive earthquakes occur in two long, twisting, and rather narrow zones. One is the Ring of Fire rimming the Pacific Ocean. The other runs from the Mediterranean Sea through the Middle East and the Himalaya Mountains, and then drops south to end among the islands of Indonesia. Both zones outline consuming boundaries.

Earthquakes occur when rocks under great strain slip and move to relieve the stress. Earthquakes along the mid-ocean ridges are relatively gentle and occur at shallow depths within the earth. This is because the material welling up at the ridges is hot and pliable. Because it is "soft," the rock beneath these ridges tends to flow rather than snap under pressure. At the consuming boundaries, however, cold edges of plate meet plate. One plate is pushed under, and it descends as a solid slab into the hot mantle. Because it is cold and rigid and can withstand much greater pressures, this slab will produce much larger earthquakes when it finally gives way under stress. You might compare earthquakes to rubber bands. The sting of a rubber band that breaks when it is stretched tight hurts more than that of a rubber band that breaks under a little tension.

Earthquakes at consuming boundaries can be unbelievably deadly. Volcanic eruptions have killed an estimated 190,000 people since A.D. 1500. But a single earthquake in 1556 killed 830,000 people in China. A 1737 quake killed 300,000 in Calcutta, India; and 143,000 died in Tokyo, Japan, in 1923 as a result of an earthquake and the fires that followed it. The worst earthquake in the United States occurred in San Francisco in 1906 and killed 452 persons.

Plate tectonics has dramatically improved scientists' understanding of what causes earthquakes and why the big ones occur where they do. And there is a strong belief that as earth scientists learn more about earthquakes that they will one day be able to predict them. Volcanologists (scientists who study volcanoes) expect that they, too, will one day be able to forecast eruptions. Right now, however, the most dependable way of predicting activity at most volcanoes is by counting earthquakes. A marked increase in the number of small, shallow tremors near a volcano often means an eruption is near.

American scientists have concentrated considerable effort on the San Andreas Fault in California, in seeking a greater understanding of earthquakes. The San Andreas is a transform boundary, where one plate grinds and scrapes past another. In the millions of years that the Pacific plate and North American plate have banged and battered together along this transform boundary, a number of smaller fractures have cracked the earth's crust. So today California is laced by faults and hit every day by small earthquakes, most of them too small to feel. Seismologists expect a quake as large as the one that devastated San Francisco in 1906 to strike California within the next century.

**The wrecked Hibernia Bank Building
in the 1906 earthquake that
damaged so much of San Francisco**

Until a few years ago most seismologists regarded earthquake prediction as an unattainable goal. But now the possibility of accurately predicting the date, the location, and the intensity of tremors appears likely. Partly through an understanding of plate tectonics, partly by discovering what happens to rocks under great strain, scientists have found that the earth gives some warning signs before a quake. Scientists in the United States and Russia have successfully predicted several small earthquakes. But they need to know far more about the clues the earth offers before earthquake predictions become reliable.

ORES AND OIL

The ideal of geology is to understand earth
as a patient and predict its behavior—
earthquakes, volcanoes, the location of mineral
and oil deposits. Earth is not a hodgepodge of
rock. It's constructed systematically. And if we
can understand that construction, we won't have
to have a lot of prospectors with their camels
and hammers out prospecting for oil and ores.
      —Geologist Robert D. Ballard of the
      Woods Hole Oceanographic Institution

In the fall of 1966 the research vessel *Chain,* from the Woods
Hole Oceanographic Institution, crisscrossed several sections of the Red Sea trying to solve a small scientific riddle.
The riddle started earlier in the decade, when oceanographers from several countries found surprisingly hot water
along the sea floor at several sites. Their readings included
one of 133 degrees Fahrenheit in a place called Atlantis II
Deep. Hot water in the ocean normally rises. So why wasn't
it doing so in the Red Sea?

Scientists from four nations aboard *Chain* concentrated
their efforts at the Atlantis II Deep. They took sediment and
water samples. They made extensive temperature measurements. What they found proved a treasure of material wealth
and scientific knowledge.

The *Chain* scientists discovered that the Atlantis II Deep
is a small basin located at a depth of about 6,600 feet. It is
in the center of the Red Sea, along the mid-ocean ridge

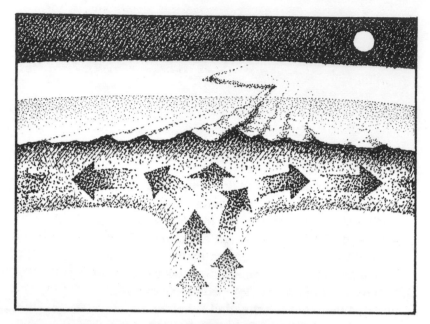

Above: Hot rock carrying minerals to the surface.
Below: Seawater seeping down through hot rock leaches
out the minerals trapped in the cooling basalt.

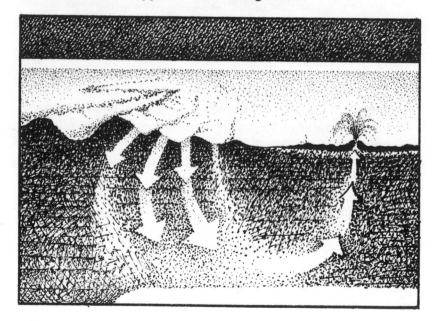

which is slowly creating an ocean out of this sea. A pool of hot brine, with high concentrations of valuable minerals dissolved in it, lies at the bottom of the basin. The weight of these metals makes the hot brine so heavy it cannot rise as normal hot water does.

The sea-floor sediments retrieved by *Chain* were even more interesting. They were among the most colorful ever taken from the oceans. Instead of the drab ooze so familiar to oceanographers, the Atlantis II Deep yielded a rainbow of colors—varying shades of white, black, red, green, blue, and yellow. And these sediments contained incredibly rich deposits of iron, manganese, zinc, copper, gold, and silver. Three hot-brine basins are now known to exist in the Red Sea, and the minerals in them are worth at least several billion dollars.

The findings from the Atlantis II Deep amazed and puzzled scientists. But in the years since, they have helped foster a deeper understanding of how plate tectonics concentrates valuable minerals and deposits them on land. Plate tectonics has also played a major role in trapping petroleum in underground pools and distributing it around the world, as geologists have discovered.

At the present time scientists can talk only in a general sense about the formation of ores and oil, and how they might be distributed. A lot more work remains before geologists can precisely pinpoint mineral and petroleum deposits, based on an understanding of plate actions. But earth scientists are confident that they will find the vital natural resources locked deep within our planet. And one day floating platforms may mine the hot-brine basins of the Red Sea and similar mineral deposits along other ocean ridges.

Geologists now believe that most of the valuable mineral deposits people mine originated along ocean ridges. At these accreting boundaries, so the current thinking goes, the hot rock from inside the earth carries copper and zinc and other metals up as it rises toward the surface. As the hot rock cools, it contracts and minute cracks open. Seawater seeps down through the rock, down more than a mile.

Seawater is rich in two chemicals, sulfur and chloride. These chemicals, under the great heat and pressure a mile beneath the surface, dissolve (or leach out) the metals trapped in the cooling basalt. After a time the seawater becomes so hot that it rises again. Eventually the water erupts through the ocean floor as hot springs or geysers. Then, as the water cools, the minerals it has brought to the surface precipitate out and fall to the ocean floor.

This is the process that is said to create the hot-brine pools and mineral-rich sediments found in the Red Sea. And in its drillings around the world, the *Glomar Challenger* has found evidence that the same process is at work along the ocean ridges in the Atlantic, Pacific, and Indian oceans. More evidence comes from the manned explorations of the Mid-Atlantic Ridge during FAMOUS. French scientists, diving in one of the fracture zones, found two deposits rich in iron and manganese. But they could find no signs of an underwater geyser that might have produced the mineral deposits. This suggests that the metals are not being produced continuously at any given spot, but that the geysers erupt only periodically.

Some sections of the ocean floor are apparently carpeted with rich mineral deposits and even veins of pure metal. Several cores drilled by the *Glomar Challenger* in the Atlantic and Indian oceans contained veins of pure copper. And evidence suggests that the island of Cyprus in the Mediterranean Sea, one of the world's oldest and richest copper mining regions, once lay on the sea floor. Geologists believe Cyprus formed as a piece of the lithosphere at an ancient mid-ocean ridge. Later, the plate buckled under pressure, and Cyprus popped up with its rich copper deposits.

Most ore deposits that are mined are not the result of plate buckling, however. Rather, they are caused by a plate's destruction. As a plate moves away from its accreting boundary, it carries its load of mineral sediments along piggyback. Millions of years later the plate is destroyed at a consuming boundary. Some of its minerals scrape off (as the descend-

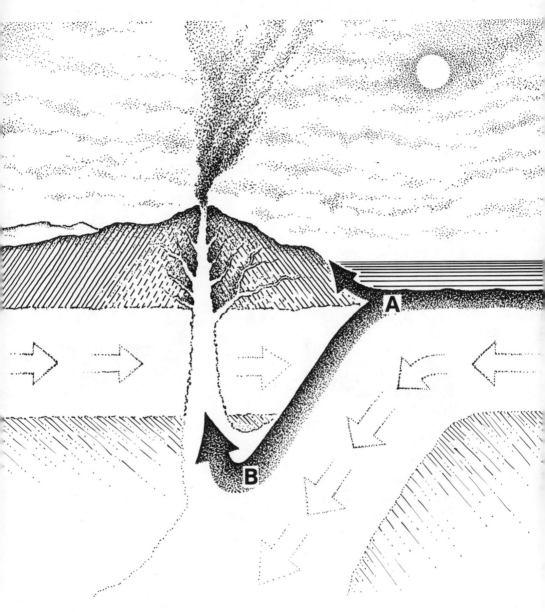

**The minerals at point A are scraped off
when one plate overrides the other.
The minerals at point B ultimately
surface through the eruption of volcanoes.**

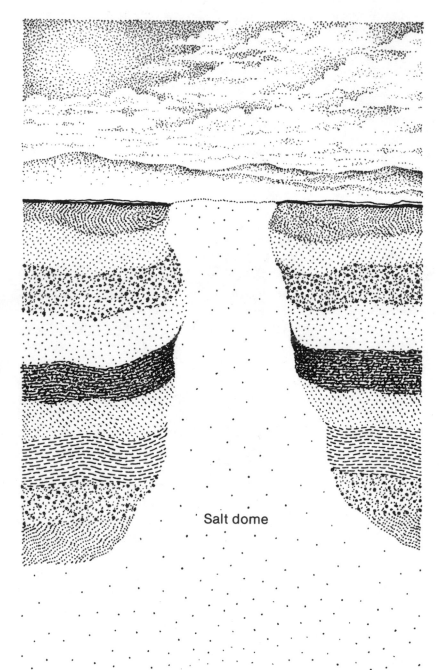

Salt dome

Salt dome rising through sedimentary rocks and oil.

ing plate rubs against the plate overriding it) and pile up as continental material. But most of the minerals, and a lot of seawater trapped in the plate's rock, plunge down with the plate. As the plate drops deeper and deeper, the heat and pressure inside the earth create the same conditions that originally brought the minerals to the surface. The seawater leaches out the minerals. Then the mineral-rich water rises to the surface, along with the molten rock that forms volcanoes. This is the way the rich ore deposits of the world formed, including those in the western United States and in the Andes of South America.

For reasons only partly understood, the various minerals are not all mixed together. Instead, they separate out and form specific deposits at different locations. Here zinc; there copper; lead elsewhere. As geologists come to understand this phenomenon better, they will be able to predict more accurately where deposits of specific minerals will be found.

Plate tectonics is also providing geologists with new clues in the world's continuing search for oil fields. Petroleum formed from the remains of plants and animals that lived tens of millions of years ago. It is a liquid, and so, like water, it can seep and flow through the ground. But to date it is useful only if it has been trapped in great underground pools that can be reached by drilling. And now geologists are finding that the movement of the earth's plates creates the geological features that trap petroleum into pools.

The breaking up of a continent provides one opportunity. As the landmass splits, a shallow sea develops first. Great layers of salt may form and be deposited along with organic matter from dead animals and plants. As the ocean opens wider, because of the spreading of the plates along an ocean ridge, the salt formations are carried away to either side. The organic matter turns to petroleum, which is trapped in large domes in the salt. If oil is found on one side of an ocean, the argument goes, it should exist on the opposite side.

The idea has worked already. By knowing where petroleum or mineral deposits existed on one side of an ocean, and by figuring out how the continents once fitted together, geologists have located a few oil and ore deposits on the other side of the ocean. But this very practical application of plate tectonics remains in its infancy. More basic knowledge must be acquired before geologists can fully exploit their understanding of plate movements to tap the vast wealth of natural resources that the earth holds hidden away.

THE FUTURE

The theory of plate tectonics, which evolved through the work of scientists in many countries, has provided great insights into the geologic history of the planet earth. Scientists have succeeded in reconstructing the movement of the continents over millions of years. They know, with good approximation, when various parts of the Atlantic Ocean opened. They have charted the slow march of India to its crushing rendezvous with Asia. They have mapped the wanderings of Antarctica, Australia, and New Zealand. And they have looked into the future and attempted to predict what will happen millions of years from now. As the plates continue their relentless movements, continents will shift and collide, new mountains will rise, and the face of the world's oceans will change dramatically.

Ten million years from now the area that is Los Angeles will probably lie alongside San Francisco. Although the two California cities are currently some 350 miles apart, they ride on top of different plates. Los Angeles is part of the Pacific plate, which is creeping northwestward along the San Andreas Fault. San Francisco rests on the North American plate and is inching to the southeast. And so, if the two plates continue moving as they are now, the two cities will meet one day.

And after that?

Three researchers at the University of Chicago sought to answer that question. Graduate student Greg Forbes, geologist Alfred Ziegler, and meteorologist Theodore Fujita calculated the plate movements. Based on their calculations, they produced a map of how the globe will look 50 million years from now. And they offered some predictions on how the changes in geography will change the earth's weather patterns. According to their predictions:

Fifty million years from now Los Angeles will be part of a long, narrow island in the Pacific Ocean that rides atop the Pacific plate. Today the land that will form this island runs from just southwest of San Francisco south to the peninsula in Mexico known as Baja California. As the Pacific plate moves northwestward, it will pull the land west of the San Andreas Fault free from North America.

The plate movements will continue to widen the Atlantic Ocean and narrow the Pacific Ocean. And 50 million years from now North America and Asia will be joined, linked where Alaska and Russia will have pushed together and closed the Bering Strait. The Kamchatka Peninsula, now a giant thumb of Russia thrust into the Pacific Ocean, will have separated from Asia and become an island. Australia will have moved northward across the equator, which will lie just north of Brisbane.

The Red Sea will be wider. A great gulf of water will curve up into East Africa where a landlocked rift valley now exists. The process of plate tectonics is splitting Africa apart in the valley, and one day ocean waters will exist where only land lies now.

The African plate's northward thrust will etch a new face of Europe and the Middle East. Africa and Europe will meet at the Strait of Gibraltar, raising a new mountain chain where the strait now stands and landlocking the Mediterranean Sea. The Persian Gulf will have vanished, destroyed by Arabia in its movement north. The collision of the Arabian plate with the Eurasian plate will build a new range of high mountains running from present-day Greece almost to the Himalayas.

These continental changes will redirect the paths of the great ocean currents, such as the Gulf Stream in the North Atlantic and the Kuroshio Current in the North Pacific. These currents greatly influence the earth's weather by the way they carry heat from the tropics to the northern and southern regions. As they change their present routes of flow, weather and climate changes will follow.

Forbes, Ziegler, and Fujita expect that tornadoes will become as common in England, France, Germany, Poland, and parts of western Russia as they are in the central United States. These countries rarely suffer tornado damage now. China and Korea, too, will suffer greatly from twisters. More hurricanes will lash the Caribbean islands, the nations bordering the Gulf of Mexico, and Brazil. But the western Pacific will experience fewer typhoons, because Australia will then cover much of the ocean area where typhoons now form.

New England and the eastern coast of Canada will be colder. But eastern Greenland, Iceland, England, Scandinavia, and the Arctic coast of European Russia will be warmer. All this because of changes in the flow of the Gulf Stream. And the Mediterranean countries will suffer colder winters because the landlocked sea will be smaller and thus less able to provide a buffer against cold air from the north.

Other scientists have tried to predict continental movements, and in some regards their maps differ from that of Forbes, Ziegler, and Fujita. Some expect Central America to disappear within the next 50 million years, separating North and South America again. Some expect that East Africa will have totally separated from the rest of the continent by then and become a large island. And some see the Red Sea opening all the way into the Mediterranean, and Africa and Europe separating wider at the Strait of Gibraltar, recreating the ancient Tethys Sea.

Predictions beyond 50 million years become even more difficult. But John Sutton of the Imperial College in London, England, for one, expects that ultimately the drifting, shifting continents will reunite once again. A new Pangaea will be born, perhaps 200 million years from now. It will be the reverse of the old. China and the western regions of the

United States and Canada, which formed part of the coastline of the old Pangaea, will be at the center of the new. The eastern United States and western Africa, which separated to begin the breakup of the old Pangaea, will form part of the coastline of the new supercontinent. And then, perhaps, the restless plates will break apart the new Pangaea, and raft its fragments once again about the face of the earth.

The theory of plate tectonics has revitalized the science of geology and given the rest of the earth sciences new life as well. It has provided a unifying explanation for many of the long-puzzling geologic phenomena of our planet—the shifting continents, the birth and death of oceans, the formation of mountains, the eruptions of volcanoes, and earthquakes. It has given new insights into the way minerals and petroleum deposits form and where they might best be sought.

Rarely in science has a single theory won such rapid acceptance and explained so much. The changes it has wrought in geology are comparable to those that followed the contributions of Copernicus in astronomy, Charles Darwin in evolutionary biology, and Albert Einstein in physics.

Yet much of the earth's geologic history and activity remains a mystery waiting to be solved. When, for example, did the earth's plates begin moving? And what set them in motion? What are the forces, deep within the earth, that keep the plates moving? And what causes tectonic activity far from plate boundaries? The Rocky and Appalachian mountains are rising a fraction of an inch each year. Why? Northern Wisconsin seems to be lifting in elevation about five feet each century. Why? The largest earthquakes in the recorded history of North America occurred in 1811 in the Mississippi Valley, not along the San Andreas Fault. Why?

These are just a few of the major questions earth scientists have yet to answer. The search for a total understanding of our dynamic home, the planet earth, is only beginning.

GLOSSARY

Abyssal plains. Immense areas of flat ocean bottom that lie deep beneath the surface.

Accreting boundary. A boundary where two plates move apart and molten material and hot rock rise from deep inside the earth to form new lithosphere.

Asthenosphere. The hot rock of the upper mantle that lies below the lithosphere.

Basalt. A type of cooled lava that makes up the rock of the ocean floor.

Climatologists. Scientists who study climates.

Consuming boundary. A boundary where one plate rides over the top of another, pushing it back deep into the earth to be remelted.

Continental rocks. The lighter rocks that form the earth's continents.

Continental shelf. The comparatively shallow ocean floor that borders a continent.

Contraction theory. A theory, which dominated geologic thinking in the 1800s, that tectonic activity occurred because the earth was cooling and shrinking in size.

Convection. The mechanism by which heat circulates when a liquid or gas is heated.

Cosmologist. A scientist who studies the origin and the evolution of the universe.

Diapir. A bulge of molten material from the asthenosphere that pushes up into the lithosphere.

Earth's crust. The layer of lighter rocks that forms the earth's outer few miles.

Earth scientists. Scientists from a variety of disciplines who study the earth, its rocks, and its behavior.

Echo sounders. Devices that bounce sound signals off the sea floor. The depth of the ocean can be determined by measuring the time a signal takes to make its round trip.

Fault. A fracture in the earth's crust along which rock can move.

Fissure. A crack in the earth's surface.

Fossil. The remains of ancient plant or animal life that are preserved in the earth's crust.

Fracture zones. Long valleys on the ocean floor, most of which run at right angles to ocean ridges.

Geology. The science that studies the history of the earth by examining its rocks.

Geophysicist. A scientist who studies the interaction of the earth's materials and energy.

Gondwanaland. The southern arm of Pangaea, which contained the lands that would become South America, Africa, India, Antarctica, and Australia.

Guyot. A flat-topped undersea mountain.

Jurassic period. A geologic time period that ran from about 190 million to 135 million years ago.

Land bridges. According to one theory, now discredited, vast stretches of land that once linked various continents but later sank beneath the sea.

Laurasia. Pangaea's northern arm, which contained the lands that became North America, Europe, and Asia.

Lithosphere. The earth's solid, outer rind, composed of its crust and the uppermost mantle.

Meteorologists. Scientists who study the weather.

Mid-ocean ridge system. The chain of undersea mountains that generally lie along the center of the ocean basins; they wind for some 47,000 miles.

Oceanography. The science that studies the ocean and its behavior.

Paleomagnetics. The study of the earth's past magnetic activity.

Paleontologist. A scientist who studies the life of past geologic periods.

Pangaea. The name Alfred Wegener gave to the supercontinent that held all the continental lands some 200 million years ago.

Plate tectonics. The theory that the earth's surface is covered by enormous, rigid blocks of rock—called plates—that move slowly about the globe; new surface material seeps up from inside the earth at the ocean ridges; old material is pushed back into the earth at the ocean trenches.

Rift valley. A valley on the earth's surface that marks a deep crack in the earth's crust.

Sediments. Layers of materials on the ocean floor that build up from dirt that is washed and blown into the sea and from the remains of tiny sea organisms that have died over millions of years.

Seismologist. A scientist who studies earthquakes.

Tectonics. The branch of geology that studies the forces that cause the earth's surface to fold, drop, and rise.

Tethys. An ancient sea that was born when Laurasia and Gondwanaland separated.

Transform boundary. A boundary where the edges of two plates grind and slip past one another.

Volcanologist. A scientist who studies volcanoes.

BIBLIOGRAPHY

Books

Anderson, Alan H., Jr. *The Drifting Continents.* New York: G. P. Putnam's Sons, 1971.

Behrman, Daniel. *The New World of the Oceans: Men and Oceanography.* Boston: Little, Brown and Co., 1969.

Briggs, Peter. *200,000,000 Years Beneath the Sea: The Story of the* Glomar Challenger. New York: Holt, Rinehart and Winston, 1971.

Calder, Nigel. *The Restless Earth: A Report on the New Geology.* New York: Viking Press, 1972.

Heezen, Bruce C., and Hollister, Charles D. *The Face of the Deep.* New York: Oxford University Press, 1971.

Articles

Earthquake Information Bulletin

  Spall, Henry. "Paleomagnetism: One Key to Plate Tectonics." January/February 1973.

Engineering: Cornell Quarterly

  Bird, John M. "The Changing Mosaic of Oceans and Continents." Summer 1973.
  Isacks, Bryan L. "The Descent of Rock into the Earth's Interior." Summer 1973.

Industrial Research

  McBirney, Alexander. "Volcanoes: Dimly Understood Danger." 15 November 1974.

National Geographic

  Canby, Thomas Y. "California's San Andreas Fault." January 1973.
  Matthews, Samuel W. "This Changing Earth." January 1973.

National Observer

Young, Patrick. "Boundary of Creation." 1 June 1974.
———. "The Earth: Scientists Say Its Shell Is Cracked." 10 June 1972.
———. "A Quake Is Due At . . ." 16 June 1973.
———. "Surprise Cracks, Magnetic Rocks on Sea Floor." 23 November 1974.
———. "World's Most Active Hot Spot." 3 February 1973.

Natural History

Colbert, Edwin H. "Antarctic Fossils and the Reconstruction of Gondwanaland." January 1972.

Nature

Bellaiche, G.; Cheminee, J. L.; Francheteau, J.; Hekinian, R. R.; Le Pichon, X.; Needham, H. D.; and Ballard, R. D. "Inner Floor of the Rift Valley: First Submersible Study." 16 August 1974.
Grocott, J.; Korstgard, J. A.; Nash, D.; and Watterson, J. "Tectonic Implications of Precambrian Shear Belts in Western Greenland." 17 April 1975.
Sillitoe, Richard H. "Tectonic Segmentation of the Andes: Implications for Magmatism and Metallogeny." 16 August 1974.
Smith, Peter J. "Oceanic Lithosphere Thickens with Age." 10 January 1975.

New York Times Magazine

Sullivan, Walter. "The Restless Continents." 12 January 1975.

NOAA Magazine

Anderson, Susan H. "Man's First Look at the Mid-Ocean Ridge." January 1975.

Oceanus

The entire Winter 1973–1974 issue.

Science

Dickinson, William R. "Plate Tectonics in Geologic History." 8 October 1971.
Eaton, Gordon P., et al. "Magma Beneath Yellowstone National Park." May 23, 1975.
Hammond, Allen L. "Plate Tectonics: The Geophysics of the Earth's Surface." 2 July 1971.
———. "Plate Tectonics (II): Mountain Building and Continental Geology." 9 July 1971.

Metz, William D., and Hammond, Allen L. "Geodynamics Report: Exploiting the Earth Sciences Revolution." 22 February 1974.

Molnar, Peter, and Tapponnier, Paul. "Cenozoic Tectonics of Asia: Effects of a Continental Collision." August 8, 1975.

Science News

Eberhart, Jonathan. "Ever Downward Beneath the Ocean Deep." 4 January 1975.

"The Mighty Amazon Reveals Her Age." 11 January 1975.

"Sea Floor Drilled to Record Depth." 3 August 1974.

Scientific American

Dewey, John F. "Plate Tectonics." May 1972.

Hallam, A. "Continental Drift and the Fossil Record." November 1972.

Heezen, Bruce C., and MacGregor, Ian D. "The Evolution of the Pacific." November 1973.

McKenzie, D. P., and Sclater, J. G. "The Evolution of the Indian Ocean." May 1973.

"Plates, Plumes, and Blobs." July 1973.

Rona, Peter A. "Plate Tectonics and Mineral Resources." July 1973.

Wyllie, Peter J. "The Earth's Mantle." March 1975.

Heirtzler, J. R., and Bryan, W. B. "The Floor of the Mid-Atlantic Rift." August 1975.

Smithsonian

Alexander, Tom. "Plate Tectonics Has a Lot to Tell Us About the Present and Future Earth." February 1975.

————. "A Revolution Called Plate Tectonics Has Given Us a Whole New Earth." January 1975.

Technology Review

Emery, Kenneth O. "New Opportunities for Offshore Petroleum Exploration." March/April 1975.

Hurley, Patrick M. "Plate Tectonics and Mineral Deposits." March/April 1975.

"A Landmark in the Earth Sciences." February 1975.

INDEX

ABOUT THE AUTHOR

Patrick Young is a staff writer for *The National Observer,* specializing in science and medical reporting. In 1970 he won the Howard W. Blakeslee Award, given by the American Heart Association, and in 1973 he received the American Society of Abdominal Surgeons Journalism Award. He is also the 1974 winner of the American Institute of Physics–United States Steel Foundation Science Writing Award in Physics and Astronomy, and he received an honorable mention in the 1974 American Association for the Advancement of Science–Westinghouse science-writing awards. Mr. Young is a member of the National Association of Science Writers. His articles on science have appeared in *Harper's Magazine* and *Saturday Review.*

Mr. Young was born in Ladysmith, Wisconsin, and graduated from the University of Colorado, *cum laude* in political science. He now lives in Laurel, Maryland, with his wife, Leah, a reporter for the *Journal of Commerce,* and their daughter, Justine. Their family beagle, Orion, is named after the Apollo 16 lunar lander.